MUSICAL VARIATIONS ON JEWISH THOUGHT

MUSICAL VARIATIONS ON JEWISH THOUGHT

OLIVIER REVAULT D'ALLONNES

INTRODUCTION
BY HAROLD BLOOM

TRANSLATED FROM THE FRENCH BY
JUDITH L. GREENBERG

GEORGE BRAZILLER / NEW YORK

Published in the United States in 1984 by George Braziller, Inc.

Originally published in France under the title
Musiques. Variations sur la pensée juive
Copyright © Christian Bourgois editeur, 1979
Introduction copyright © 1983 by Harold Bloom
English translation copyright © 1983 by George Braziller, Inc.

For information address the publisher:
    George Braziller, Inc.
    One Park Avenue
    New York, NY 10016

Library of Congress Cataloging in Publication Data
Revault d'Allonnes, Olivier.
    Musical variations on Jewish thought.
    Includes bibliographical references.
    1. Judaism—Essence, genius, nature.   2. Jews—
Psychology.   3. Abraham (Biblical patriarch)   I. Title.
BM565.R4713   1983   296'.01   83—15640
ISBN 0-8076-1080-1

Printed in the United States of America

First Printing

INTRODUCTION

I

Freud speculated that what we first forget, and only subsequently remember, is the most important element in a dream, or perhaps in any other representation of our desires. "Important" here means what is central for an interpretation. Freud's theory of *repression*, or unconscious yet purposeful forgetting, is at the center of his vast speculative project. Consequently, we know a great deal about Freudian forgetting, yet remarkably little about what might be termed Freudian remembering. Since Freud's was anything but a psychology of historical changes, we might have expected that his view of people as immutable through the ages would have concerned itself with what most makes for the immutable, which is memory and its discontents. If we have an unchanging nature, then the past should have unchallenged authority for us. But Freud's therapeutic design intends the undoing of our histories. Not only is individual sexuality to be liberated from the family romance, but thought itself is to be freed of its necessarily sexual past— freed at least in a few, elite individuals strong enough to bear their own freedom.

Freud refused to study the nostalgias. He hated the past, and he hated the United States, perhaps because he feared that it was the future. But his hatred of America was founded upon ignorance, while he *knew* the past, and so hated it with reason. Jews are urged by their tradition to *remember*, but very selectively. Freud was peculiarly Jewish, in profound ways that we begin only now to understand. Olivier Revault d'Allonnes shrewdly notes and commends Freud's ingenuity in having transformed the initial prime obstacle to psychoanalysis, the transference, into the pragmatic prime instrument of analytical therapy. If there is something ineluctably Jewish about that transformation, then perhaps we can take it as a synecdoche for all the Jewish metamorphoses of exile into achievement. The wandering people has taught itself and others the lesson of wandering meaning, a wandering that has compelled a multitude of changes in the modes of interpretation available to the West. Of these changes, the Freudian speculation has been perhaps the most influential in our century, if only because we now find it difficult to recall that psychoanalysis, after all, is only a speculation, rather than a science, a philosophy, or even a religion. Freud is closer to Proust than to Einstein, closer even to Kafka than to the scientism of Darwin.

What marks the Freudian transference, above all, is ambivalence, which is also the particular mark of Freud's mythological version of the taboo (in his seminal cultural speculation, *Totem and Taboo*). Ambivalence, in Freud's sense, is simultaneous love and hatred directed toward the same object. The transference and the taboo alike are variations upon Freud's central vision of psychic ambivalence, the Oedipus complex. Transforming an obstacle to analysis into a technique of analysis is therefore equivalent to converting the Oedipal intensities from a human burden into a human release. If this element in Freudian *praxis* truly is indebted to the wisdom of the Diaspora, in very broad cultural terms, then Freud is another of the authors of the Jewish myths of Exile, and psychoanalysis becomes another parable of a people always homeless or at least uneasy in space, who must seek a perpetually deferred fulfillment in time.

Whether there is a specifically biblical basis for the Jewish discontent with visual space, and the Jewish creative obsession with hearing in time, is disputable. Most attempts to contrast Hebrew and Greek thought, on the supposed basis of crucial differences between Hebrew and Greek as languages, have been demonstrated to be illusory. Yet the intellectual and spiritual conflict between Jew and Greek is anything but illusory, and indeed still seems irreconcilable. Western conceptualization is Greek, and yet Western religion, however conceptualized, is not. Freud curiously reduced *all* religion to the longing for the father. Whatever we may think of this reduction, it is not Greek. Nor is the Freudian Eros at all Greek, since Freud interprets every investment of libido as a transaction in the transference of authority, which always resides in figures of the individual's past and only rarely survives in the individual proper. It is not Greek to vacillate between the need to be everything in oneself and the anxiety of being nothing in oneself. That vacillation helps account for what Freud called repression or defense, the flight from forbidden representations of desire. The theory of repression is coherent only in a psychic cosmos where absolutely everything is meaningful, so that a dream or a joke or a symptom or a transference can sustain a level of interpretative intensity akin to the rabbinical procedures for unpacking Torah. "Turn it and turn it, for everything is in it," the sage Ben Bag Bag remarks of Torah in *Pirke Abot*. This aphorism could have served as epigraph to Freud's *The Interpretation of Dreams*

(*Traumdeutung*), but only because Freud, like the rabbis, had placed everything in the past.

To ask whether there is a specifically Jewish attitude toward time is to ask the even more problematical question: What is it to be Jewish? Does one intend the biblical, or the normatively rabbinical, or something more belated by the question? Three thousand, and more, years of apparent continuity mask astonishing discontinuities, as many of them ancient as modern. The clearest answer ought to be religious, but the phrase "the Jewish religion" is itself misleading. Generally, the phrase refers to what the Harvard historian of religion, George Foot Moore, first named "normative Judaism": the faith of Akiba and his colleagues in the second century of the Common Era. But they lived perhaps twelve centuries after the Yahwist, greatest and most original of the biblical writers. Between his tales of Abraham, Jacob, Joseph and Moses, and the rabbis' extraordinary modes of interpretation, there had been many interventions, of which the most decisive was the influx of Greek culture after Alexander's world conquests. The Oral Torah, created by the rabbis as a defensive hedge around Scripture, is ultimately Platonic in its function, though not in its ideology. Nothing in the Hebrew Bible proclaims the holiness of study, or sees the Jewish people saving themselves, as a people, by Torah learning. Yet this vision of sanctification through instruction has become so Judaic, even so Jewish, that its Platonic origin now constitutes a shock for almost all Jews, however scholarly. The historical difference between the Yahwist and Akiba *is* Plato, and this influx of Athens into Jerusalem saved Judaism, and the Jews, from being scattered into oblivion among the nations, by giving the Jews a central formulation of their own culture, but in Greek, the universal language.

Differences between Hebrew and Greek ideas of history nevertheless abound, though whether those differences can aid us in separating out distinctive Jewish notions of time and of memory is problematical. Revault d'Allonnes has composed a musical reverie rather than a historical meditation, but his work can be illuminated by Yosef Hayim Yerushalmi's *Zakhor: Jewish History and Jewish Memory* (1982). The Hebrew Bible commands the Jews to remember, because its God is primarily "the God of your fathers, the God of Abraham, Isaac and Jacob," known only through His historical self-revelations, rather than through the cycles of time, natural or mythic. Historical time as such does not matter to Israel; what matters are the times when God intervenes and Israel responds. Significant time, in this sense, is clearly not a Greek notion, for a surprising reason that has more to do with "Israel responds" than "God intervenes." What is peculiarly Judaic is the faith that God's interventions are always primarily for the purpose of eliciting Israel's response. In this sense also, the Freudian view of the human predicament remains biblical. Because the intervention is for *our* response, we can be tempted to believe we are everything; because the intervener is incommensurate with us, we can fear that we are nothing. The Psalms echo with this most terrible of affective self-contradictions, taking us in a few phrases from lying down among the potsherds to being as the wings of a dove. It is the biblical and now the Freudian view of man that is Shakespearean also, rather than the Roman stoicism of Seneca. Hamlet's dramatic reveries transcend even the Yahwist and Freud in a dialectical awareness that everything, and yet nothing, is for Hamlet's sake alone.

Yerushalmi is rightly skeptical of any rigid distinctions that posit radically contrasting modes of perceiving time in Greek and Hebrew ways of thinking. Linguistic structures and semantic histories do not yield valid clues to biblical thought, as James Barr's *Biblical Words for Time* (1969) demonstrated against John Marsh's *The Fullness of Time* (1952) and Thorleif Boman's *Hebrew Thought Compared with Greek* (1960). Boman in particular has argued for a sharp cleavage between Greek and Hebrew perceptions of time, even insisting that the Greeks valued space over time, a valorization founded upon the sense of seeing as the prime sense for experiencing existence, which he contrasts to the Hebraic emphasis upon hearing. Setting aside Boman's rather dubious linguistic thesis, some such contrast may still be valid if we restrict ourselves to encounters with divinities. Certainly the gods of the Greeks have more spatial than temporal authority, while the Jewish God declares His own reality as a dialectic of presence in time. *Ehyeh asher ehyeh*, God says to Moses, mistranslated as "I Am that I Am" but more accurately rendered as "I Will be [present when and where] I Will be." God's presence is attested by his word (*davar*), while the Word of God is hardly a Greek concept as such. The great rabbinical apothegm concerning God—"He is the place (*makom*) of the world, but the world is not His place"—defines the difference. How odd it would have sounded to a Greek: "Zeus is the place of the world, but the world is not his place." And even odder, to the Jews, would have been: "God is the time of the world, but the world is not His time."

The contrast between a Greek exaltation of space and the Hebraic esteem for time was set forth most suggestively by Nietzsche, when in *Thus Spake Zarathustra* he defined the Jews as the people that honored their father and their mother, and the Greeks as the nation that strove for excellence, for occupying the foremost place. The Greek *agon* is thus for an individual dominance in personal space, as it were, whether in civic power or in poetry. To honor one's parents, and *their* parents, and all the parents back to Abraham and Sarah, is to contend only for the Blessing, which is temporal, partaking in *olam*, which can be rendered as "time without boundaries." When Jacob wrestles all night with a nameless angel, the struggle is not for a place, but *to delay the angel*, whose temporal anxiety is overwhelming: "Let me go, for it is daybreak!" The angel is not God (a Protestant misreading) but perhaps the Angel of Death, and Jacob's victory depends upon the angel's refusal to confront the dawn. Space is therefore secondary, in contrast to the catastrophic combat between Oedipus and Laius at the crossroads, which concerns yielding place. Blessed by the new name of Israel, Jacob limps away from Penuel, with the sun rising upon *him*, but not upon the supernatural being who has fled. Israel's limp testifies to having been crippled at a particular place, but the far more vital testimony is to the triumph of having prevailed into a time without boundaries.

For Revault d'Allonnes, the crucial Jewish antithesis is between time in history and time in music—or Blake's "pulsation of an artery," in which the poet's and the composer's work is done. This most audacious and winning trope in the reverie of Revault d'Allonnes is securely based upon biblical precedents, for the time of the Patriarchs and the Prophets is surely closer to music than to history, which is to say that Jewish time is founded upon a peculiar version of memory. Yerushalmi reminds us that certain lengthy reigns of biblical monarchs are dismissed with the briefest of formulas: "He did evil in the sight of the Lord." What matters is what is judged to be memorable, and Israel's response to the word of God is the test by which history is converted into memory, or is set aside forever. Memory is what *was heard in time*, whether by Israel or, in Revault d'Allonnes, by Isaiah and by Beethoven. The literal deafness of Beethoven thus implicitly becomes analogous to the rabbinical deafness toward those historical figures who would not hear God in time.

2

It is by a certain curious sense of interiority that Revault d'Allonnes links music and Jewish thought, as two modes that negate all idolatry, all bondage to the bodily eye. The invisible God of the Jews makes only a handful of actual appearances in the Bible, and in only one of those—the Sinai theophany, where the elders sit, eat and gaze at Him—does He fail to speak. Appearances count for less in the Bible than in very nearly any other literature, and there must be some connection, however obscured by our estrangement from the Bible, between this devaluation of the eye and the extraordinary text of the Second Commandment:

> You shall not make for yourself a sculptured image, or any likeness of what is in the heavens above, or on the earth below, or in the waters under the earth. For I the Lord your God am an impassioned God, visiting the guilt of the fathers upon the children, upon the third and upon the fourth generations of those who reject Me, but showing kindness to the thousandth generation of those who love Me and keep My commandments.

This zealous or impassioned God molded Adam in His own *zelem* (image) and so presumably He is urging us not to presume to emulate Him, that being the Greek sin of Prometheus or the Romantic sin of Frankenstein. But the prohibition then continues until it becomes remarkably comprehensive, and the Divine passion mounts to Sublime hyperbole. That the intent of the Second Commandment is to compel us to an extreme interiority is palpable enough, but the very power of this rhetoric encouraged the rebellious Gnostic imagination to an unprecedented originality in the idolatry of fabulation. For Revault d'Allonnes as for Walter Pater, all art and indeed all speculation aspires to the condition of music, a mode apart from idolatry. Revault d'Allonnes does not refer to the preferred Biblical way of representing an object, which is to explain *how it was made*. Boman notes that we are not told how the Ark, the Desert Sanctuary, the Temple and Solomon's Palace looked, because the stories of how they were built is what constitutes depiction. And though we are told that Joseph, David and Absalom were outstandingly handsome, again we are given only an impression, with no sense of their actual appearance. Yet the beauty of Absalom is hardly an index to his interiority, except in ways so subtle as to suggest that the great writer who composed II Samuel had his own highly original doubt of appearances. The Second Commandment evidently was no inhibition for prose narrative, and perhaps we are wrong to find in it the ancestor of many of the later Jewish anxieties of representation.

Yet some of these do have profound if dialectical connections to the rabbinical tradition, which as Walter Benjamin remarked, chose *not to see*, a legacy he rightly found a memory still alive in Kafka, and which seems to me equally lively in Freud's theories. Revault d'Allonnes is sensitive to the place of the Negative in Jewish thought, a sensitivity upon which I wish to expand. Do Freud and Kafka manifest a Jewish version of negation, one highly distinct from the Hegelian mode of negative thinking? Hegelian negation both culminates European rationalism and aggressively sets that rationalism against British empiricism, with its contempt for universals. Herbert Marcuse observed that Hegel's intellectual optimism is based upon a destructive concept of the given, thus denying any empirical insistence upon the ultimate authority of the fact. Freudian *Verneinung* is anything but a Hegelian dialectical negation, alien to Freud both in its optimism and in its transcendence of mere fact. Rather, Freud's Negative is dualistic, mingling ambivalently a purely cognitive return of the repressed, and a continuation of the repression of all affect, of the flight away from forbidden and yet desired images and memories. We can call Hegelian negation perhaps the most profound of all Gentile idealizations, after Plato, and then say of the Freudian (and Kafkan) mode of negation that always it reenacts the ambiguities of the Second Commandment.

Revault d'Allonnes implicitly recognizes this, and following his reveries can help us to see that the difference between Hegelian and Freudian *Verneinung* is evaded by French Freudians (Lacan, Deleuze, Laplanche, even Derrida). This evasion invalidates their readings of Freud, since ultimately they destroy his proud dualisms by rendering them into mere "psychical duplicities"

(O. Mannoni, Lacanian ephebe). Hegelian negation allows the mind to attain the self-consciousness that will free nature, history, and society from the authority of empiricism and positivism. So Marcuse sums up Hegelian truth as "the result of a double process of negation, namely, (1) the negation of the 'per se' existence of the object, and (2) the negation of the individual I with the shifting of the truth to the universal." But Freud, as Richard Wollheim writes, "traced . . . the capacity to assign truth or falsity to an assertion, to some very primitive movement of the mind, in which something like a thought is felt within one," and then it is either projected or introjected. This is certainly not Hegelian, but is very close to what Yerushalmi calls "Jewish memory."

Hegelianizing Freud, whether in the linguistic mode of Lacan or the subtler, more skeptical way of Derrida, ends by undoing his radical dualisms (Primary Process/Secondary Process; Pleasure Principle/Reality Principle), and by thus driving Freud into a kind of phantasmagoric monism, in which the primal ambivalence of an aggressive narcissism becomes our ruling passion. But if you undo Freud's dualisms, then you confound him with his "renegades"—Jung, Adler, Reich, Rank, all of them what the poet Wallace Stevens called "fundamentalists of the First Idea." True, Freud's First Idea of civil war in the psyche still would be conflictive, but the conflict will tend to take place *within* a narcissistic, mostly unconscious ego, rather than between the ego and the superego, or the ego and the id. That is as large a revision of Freud as Adler was, and if my surmises are accurate, it also removes Freud from the problematical domain of Jewish memory.

Revault d'Allonnes engagingly locates Freud in that domain by first acknowledging "the often contradictory and ambiguous relationship between Freud and Judaism," but then subtly associating the biblical and the Freudian ideas of personality and the possibilities of its sublimation. I would add to Revault d'Allonnes that sublimation, in the Freudian sense, may well be a Jewish ideal, but the true center of Freud's work is the concept of repression, which is profoundly Jewish, and even normatively so. Freudian memory is Jewish memory, and Freudian forgetting is yet more Jewish. Freud's *Verdrängung* is now weakly translated by "repression," whose current Western overtones are misleadingly ideological and even political. But *Verdrängung*, despite its etymology, is not the trope of pushing under or pushing down, but rather the trope of flight, of an estrangement from representations, under the influence of an inner drive.

I come full circle here by returning to the idea of a psychic cosmos, rabbinical and Freudian, in which there is sense in everything, be-

cause everything already is in the past, and
nothing that matters can be utterly new. Rabbinical memory, as Yerushalmi expounds it, insists
that all meanings are present already in the Bible, in its normative commentaries, and in the oral
law represented in each generation by the inter-
preters who stand centrally in the tradition. If
everything is there already, then everything in the
Bible is absolutely meaningful. Mix together this
passion for total intelligibility with a discarding
of every mythology, of all idolatry, of the possibility of mere irrationalisms, and you are very
close to Freud's own stance regarding individual
consciousness (memory). This must be why Freud
had the audacity, in the special preface he wrote
for the Hebrew version of *Totem and Taboo*, to
affirm the inward Jewishness of his science, and
to hint even that he might be forming a Judaism
for the future. The Second Commandment, in our
time, is called Primal Repression, which now takes
place before there is anything to be repressed.

3

A people obsessed by time, selectively remembering, while always unconsciously yet purpose-
fully forgetting whatever their own inwardness
cannot negate—this seems the description of a

tale by Kafka, perhaps not quite "Josephine the Singer and the Mouse Folk," yet near enough. Kafka's unfinished books prophesy the stance of Edmond Jabès: "For the Jew, having a place means finishing a book. / The unfinished book was our survival." When the Messianic hope, however nuanced, is unavailable, then the Bible gives the illusion of being finished, and the survival of the Jews *as Jews* finally is put into question, which means that Jewish memory hesitates, as though nearing its end. Without texts, and in particular *the* text, the Jews vanish. Doubtless the New Testament and the Koran are as central for their faiths, but the continued existence of a people does not altogether turn upon them. The ancient formulation retains its force: not the Book of the people, but the people of the Book. But what is it to be "of the Book"? Set religion aside. Perhaps the normative rabbis of the Second Century, Common Era, of the Age of Akiba, were religious, as now we use the word, but what is strongest in the Hebrew Bible is not the work of "religious writers." The Yahwist, strongest writer in the Bible, is far too uncanny and idiosyncratic to be named a religious writer. To be "of the Book" of the Yahwist, of the author of II Samuel or of Jeremiah or Job is to be of writers as original and peculiar as Dante, Chaucer, Shakespeare, Milton. A Scripture hardly need be an aesthetic glory to be of permanent religious influence; much of the New Testament is weak writing, and the Book of Mormon is nearly as opaque as the Revelation of John the Divine. But peoples are molded by preternaturally strong writers: the Yahwist, Homer, Shakespeare. The ancient Jews were not first a people and then a religion, but that odder phenomenon, a religion that became a people. Revault d'Allonnes engagingly relies upon his trope of nomadism. It leads him to the one insistence in his book that puzzles me: his distinction, following Renan, between Elohim and Yahweh, with the preference given to Elohim, as the supposed authentic deity of nomadism, of freedom. Neither historical scholarship nor a perceptive literary criticism sustains Renan's point; the Yahwist *was* the original author, and the Elohist only an anxious revisionist, if even so much as that. And the texts of Yahweh, and not those where God is called Elohim, are almost always the great texts, the stories that created a people. Revault d'Allonnes defends his preference for a nomadic Elohim as being his own romantic dream. An unassailable defense, but I advise the reader to meet it by an accurate substitution. Yahweh, uncanny and unconditioned, is truly the God of what Revault d'Allonnes praises as Jewish nomadism, and the people of the Book are as much the people of the Yahwist as the Greeks were of Homer and as the English still are of Shakespeare.

Freud implicitly knew this, and that knowledge underlies his weird late book, *Der Mann Moses und die monotheistiche Religion* (*The Man Moses*, translated into English as *Moses and Monotheism*). In what Freud himself called "my novel," the Yahwist is so revised as to vanish, and Moses is declared to be an Egyptian, Yahwism thus becoming an Egyptian invention. Freud's motives were at least double: to revitalize the outrageous Primal History Scene of *Totem and Taboo*, and to remove a major rival for authority. It is worth remarking that Freud eagerly speculated, at just this time, that the Earl of Oxford had written Shakespeare, a curious devaluation of yet another true rival. Though dismissing this "cultural" Freud of totemism and of an Egyptian Moses might be a comfort, the dismissal would have to be uneasy, both because the figurative power of the Primal History Scene lingers, and because the taboo-and-totem complex is the concealed paradigm for the Freudian therapeutics of the transference.

Nothing could be less Jewish than the Primal History Scene, which reads like a parody of Blake's *Tiriel*, and which centers upon a primal horde of rival brothers, who combine to murder and devour their terrible father, who has taken all the women of the horde for his own. Once slain and digested, the father becomes a venerated ancestor god, Nietzsche's "numinous shadow" of *The Genealogy of Morals*. Ambivalence having been resolved by this grotesquely literal introjection of the father, remorse for the crime against the father begins—a remorse upon which, Freud insists, all culture is founded. Religion, Judaism included, is thus the desire for the dead father, whose name in Judaism alternately might be Yahweh or Moses, or for some among us now, Sigmund Freud. The dead father, our father Freud remarked, proved mightier than the living one had been. But Yahweh (*contra* the preference of Renan and Revault d'Allonnes for Elohim) was the true name of the father: Baal and Moloch were not fathers, and Jesus Christ perpetually is a son and not a brother of Yahweh. Freud's grandest heresy, from a Judaic perspective, is his transfer of the Hebraic trope of the fatherhood of Yahweh to the hideous totemic ancestor god of the primal horde. Yahweh's elective love for Israel, the center of all Jewish memory, could not be more at variance with the Freudian account of our erotic attachment to authority: in Freud authority has no love for us.

Freedom, for Freud, had to be freedom from the past, but never from time, wherein Revault d'Allonnes locates the Jewish (and Freudian) reality principle. Pragmatically, Jewish freedom is freedom of interpretation, though Jewish (and Freudian) memory results in all meaning being overdetermined. What *is* freedom where everything is overdetermined, where character is fate, and there are, after all, no accidents? Freud's scientism, not his Jewishness, led to his proud embrace of the reductive, but his path out of his own reductionism proved to be his quite Jewish variety of dualism. Revault d'Allonnes states the essence of Judaism to be the desire for justice, against the world, and the related inwardness of morality such desire creates. Prophetic dualism is precisely that: Elijah and Amos stand against the unjust world, and so against all outwardness whatsoever. But this at last is Freud's dualism also: the psyche is at civil war, but what it wars with, in itself, is the injustice of outwardness, the defensive disorderings of the drives, the unnecessary sufferings that rob us of the freedom that yet can be our time.

This freedom Freud named "negation," and I turn again to this difficult formulation in his very brief, almost abrupt paper of that title in 1925. Negation works so as to internalize certain objects of the drive, an internalization that ensues in the very difficult trope of "the bodily ego," which in each of us can be regarded as the object of our own id. But an "internalized object" is an even more difficult trope or fiction, justified because Freud's extraordinary ambition is to seek to explain nothing less than the origins of thinking, indeed of thinking as a relatively free process. How can a thought become an object, even if that object has been swallowed up by one's bodily ego? Following Revault d'Allonnes, I would say that Freud has found a complex metaphor, in the essence of Jewishness, for the ambivalently mingled introjection and projection that together constitute his concept of Negation. Combine a moral obsession with justice, and the drive to a progressively greater inwardness, and you get what Freud might have called "the bodily superego," or the personified prophetic conscience, or the nomadic Jew of Revault d'Allonnes.

4

The moment in his reverie that perhaps most moves d'Allonnes himself is when he has a vision of God, on the first Sabbath, taking time for Himself by listening to music. The Jewish God is a personality and a subjectivity, and only if indeed He *is* dead, is the death of the subject more than a currently fashionable Gallic trope. Revault d'Allonnes cites Spinoza's wholly Jewish apothegm: "Wisdom is meditation not on death but on life." Either writer might have quoted the fundamental Jewish admonition of the rabbi Tarphon, in *Pirke Abot*: "You are not required to complete the work, but neither are you free to desist from it." The work cannot be completed in time, yet we must work as if there will be time enough to complete it, "to give time to time," as in the Sephardic proverb that Revault d'Allonnes repeats. Judaism, never much interested in death, is in consequence hardly a philosophical religion, if philosophy be the study of death. Jacob, who won the name Israel, is in my judgment the most Jewish figure in the Bible, because of his endless struggle for the Blessing, which in every sense primarily means *more life*.

And yet, consider what constitutes the highest spiritual achievements of modern Jewry: the speculations of Freud, the stories and parables of Kafka, the recovery of Jewish Gnosis by Gershom Scholem. Freud concludes with the vision of a primal ambivalence; Kafka makes a tendency toward ambiguity into a kind of drive; Scholem opposes to the ritual of rabbinical Judaism, which makes nothing happen, the ritual of the Lurianic Kabbalah, a ritual which is a theurgy: these are hardly celebrations of more life. In his exaltation of nomadism and redemptive time, Revault d'Allonnes risks an archaic Jewishness, perhaps too much a reverie of his own will, which is to say, his own performance of the Bible as though it were Beethoven: "The world of the Bible is not God's nightmare: It is His will intermingled with the expression of that will. The time of music in Beethoven is not the internalization of a secret of his, it is the awareness of it organized into a communicable and referential language and thereby made universal, as is the Bible."

Alas, Revault d'Allonnes idealizes here, for surely Beethoven, in these terms, is far more universal than the Bible, which is now the most recalcitrant and difficult of all libraries (we cannot call it a text, though it is text itself). Doubtless, the deep study of Beethoven brings far more to an adept musician than does even the most alert listening, yet Beethoven is available to questing listeners. The Bible is anything but universal, however we attempt to listen to it, because it addresses an elite. In the Sinai theophany, as presented by the Yahwist, we are bewildered by the emotional self-contradictions of God, at once inviting the people up to Him, and yet warning also that if they break through to Him, He may break forth against them. Beethoven does not say to us, even implicitly, "Be like me, but do not dare to be too like me!" In shying away from Yahweh, and toward the Elohim, Revault d'Allonnes evades the Biblical ambiguity that haunted Kafka, always. Revault d'Allonnes concludes: "The Bible and music give us back our lives whereas idols rob us of them. The Bible and music give consistency to the image of that life, reflecting it directly at us." Kafka, ambiguously apprehensive of biblical ambiguity, has a very different sense of how the Bible might or might not give us back our lives, as in this meditation upon the life of Moses:

> He is on the track of Canaan all his life; it is incredible that he should see the land only when on the verge of death. The dying vision of it can only be intended to illustrate how incomplete a moment is human life, incomplete because a life like this could last forever and still be nothing but a moment. Moses fails to enter Canaan not because his life is too short but because it is a human life.

Revault d'Allonnes is more in Kafka's spirit when he qualifies his own conclusion, telling us that the image of our life given by the Bible is "at once derisory and pitiless, tortured and vain," yet "fascinating to feel" because still marked by hope. Despite his nostalgia, Revault d'Allonnes is of the Age of Freud and Kafka, who may not have wanted to become Jewish culture, but who nevertheless have redefined that culture for us. *Musical Variations on Jewish Thought* is an evocative reverie, more reliant upon nuance than upon argument. Revault d'Allonnes implicitly reminds us, less historically than Yerushalmi does in *Zakhor*, that all contemporary Jewish intellectuals are compelled to recognize that they are products of a rupture with their tradition, however much they long for continuity. What could that continuity hope to be, except a form of rupture, another breaking of the vessels? We no longer know just what makes a book Jewish, or a person Jewish, because we have no authority to instruct us as to what is or is not Jewish thought. Revault d'Allonnes strongly sets himself against idolatry, but this Jewish stance raises again the problem of whether an aesthetic humanism is not one of the most available modes of idolatry—an accusation that has been made against my own work by some claiming to speak with authority in Jewish matters. I am content to entrust my own defense to the most eloquent turn in Revault d'Allonnes, when he denies that "the nomad Abraham" is submissive to God, is a mere obeyer of orders. Like Milton, like his beloved Beethoven, Revault d'Allonnes exalts creative freedom, the liberty of crossing over to God's side: "the liberty of God, who is, if one dare say so, under no obligation to extricate the races from their monotonous repetition." Again Revault d'Allonnes risks being confronted by the more-than-ironic ambiguity of Kafka:

> Abraham falls victim to the following illusion: he cannot stand the uniformity of this world. Now the world is known, however, to be uncommonly various, which can be verified at any time by taking a handful of world and looking at it closely. Thus this complaint at the uniform-

ity of the world is really a complaint at not having been mixed profoundly enough with the diversity of the world.

Since the Jews, the Christians and the Moslems are all children of Abraham, all Western religion is here slyly traced to an illusion of uniformity. What seemed monotonous repetition to Father Abraham may have been a product of his own myopia, the failure to scrutinize a handful of world closely enough. But such scrutiny always robs us of the motive for metaphor, the desire to be different, the desire to be elsewhere, which is Nietzsche's nomadic genealogy of the aesthetic impulse. Kafka's is too formidable an ambiguity to turn fairly against Revault d'Allonnes or any other modern Jewish thinker, with the single exception of Freud (unless Proust is to be claimed as another such thinker). The Kafkan ambiguity is very uneasy, when turned against Freud. To call Freud the Rashi of contemporary Jewish anxieties, as Kafka did, is to compliment even Rashi too highly.

Freud necessarily has dominated this Introduction, as inevitably he pervades all of modern Jewish thought, indeed *all* modern thought. Brooding on the Moses of Michelangelo, Freud found in the piece "a concrete expression of the highest mental achievement that is possible in a man, that of struggling successfully against an inward passion for the sake of a cause to which he has devoted himself." The inward passion here is the justified prophetic wrath that would break the Tablets of the Law, and so Freud reads in this Moses his own lineaments. What can struggle so successfully against so inward a passion is a freedom even more inward, the freedom of the Law, of Torah, "of the highest mental achievement." Revault d'Allonnes has written, not in the freedom of the Law, which is reserved for an Abraham or a Freud, but in a still traditional Jewish freedom. This once was called the freedom to move from the broken tablets to the free tablets. More modestly, and as persuasively, Olivier Revault d'Allonnes calls this freedom *Musical Variations on Jewish Thought.*

Harold Bloom

MUSICAL VARIATIONS ON JEWISH THOUGHT

Even music known by heart retains a trace of the unexpected, for the very nature of its substance, time, is what does not yet exist, what will be, what can, at any moment, become different: the music can stop, the performer miss a note, the instrument break, the musician abandon the text, or my attention begin to wander. Even the score, however imperative it might be in Western music, is only an incomplete series of guidemarks, awaiting a living being to take possession of it. In short, music is inseparable from a certain improvisation, an accessibility to the overtures of time. It is, for that reason, inseparable from liberty: never entirely committed or caught up in the instant which is coming to an end, but always open to any other. Like our life, music is revealed, little by little, in its development; like our death, it is irrevocably sealed only in silence. Or rather, it initiates movements, arouses expectations, but only the better to disappoint them.

No: surprise them. For it is precisely its unexpectedness that makes music pleasing. The "law of good form," dear to Gestaltists, applies to the spatial arts but not to music. For music's worst enemy is boredom, repetition, the foreseeable. But the converse is true and music, like an unfettered life, is the opposite of boredom. An art of time, it does not surrender or submit itself to it: music entrusts itself to time, puts its faith in it, knowing that whatever time might bring, it will bring something and will give it its existence—for a time. In that way, music is life and the open, unfettered, free life is music.

Thus a subtle but steadfast complicity appears between the musical spirit and love, respect for time and predilection for its works, from silence to tumult, from the cry of sorrow to the dance of joy, from mathematical structure to inspired delirium, from classicism to romanticism, from Mozart to Beethoven.

But are there other forms of music than music? Other ways of living freely than by listening to the liberty of time? Yes, there are, but at the opposite pole of our confinement by giant cities and their prefabricated time tables, their calendars, time clocks and fascinating and futile obligatory material objects: their idols and their power. Thus, a music lover could seek the antidote to idols only in the Bible; the following essay attempts to do so.

I will not directly consider music, or not quite. Yet, on the other hand, the essay will treat only music insofar as the ancient Hebrews will be presented as incurable nomads, even when they wanted not to be; insofar as the Bible will be perceived throughout as the saga of world without end; insofar as sensitivity to time not space will be proposed as the constant benchmark of Jewish thought and as its irreducible contribution to other systems of reference.

This essay, a product of the esthetic concern of a music lover who wonders about music and his fondness for it, boldly, with neither mastery nor modesty, passes through fields of knowledge as respectable as ethnology, history, anthropology and biblical studies. And then it ventures, not entirely deliberately, on moral and political digressions. Can it too, for that reason, legitimately claim to be music? In any case, it could have no other title.

* * *

Biblical prophetism, in its main aspect, is utopian: it describes the exigencies of justice, it announces the events by which the divinity will punish the wicked and insure the reign of the good. It even goes so far as to describe repeatedly the realization of justice for eternity. The drafters of the Bible see and describe the reality of their times: violence, cowardice, cupidity, treachery, carnal-mindedness and, above all, idolatry and impiety. But they only inveigh against the present and even pronounce the very threats of the Eternal long enough to throw into higher relief that world of tomorrow, that dream object, that millenary anticipation of those who thirst for justice.

This thirst is rooted in man's heart, the only temple worthy of Elohim, the divine principle of the Patriarchs. Here, then, in the works of the Prophets, is a vision of the world which elaborates that of the Torah, retaining in particular, and endlessly unfolding, its specifically moral aspect. Countless "scholars" have brooded over these texts without ever succeeding in elucidating them completely. So much the better. In the gaps of their scholarship, or sometimes even in place of it, with no pretense of taking its place, there is room for dreams.

Thirty centuries have attempted to understand something of biblical thought, and none has succeeded. The last two of these thirty centuries have even claimed to bring the resources of "science" to bear on the problem and their failure, if one may venture to say so, is even worse. Other ages did not elucidate the Bible, but at least their efforts, by the projection of their own obsessions, teach us something about them. Let us resume that tradition, even at the expense of renouncing organized discourse. Even if the Bible were to succeed simply in making us become aware of ourselves through the millennia, it would still have attained its aim, which is to affirm the presence of inwardness. Reverie cannot be a treacherous method, it might even be the only approach to this text which, from the invention of a single God to that of a chosen People, from Moses to Jonah and from Abraham to Joshua, is nothing but the grandiose verbalization of the dreams of a multitude.

Eight hundred and fifty years or so, then, before the so-called Christian era, anonymous writers of the kingdom of Israel and of the kingdom of Judah set about gathering in writing the legends of their people, without knowing, of course, that some of them, such as the legend of Adam and Eve in the earthly paradise, are from Babylon and others, such as the flaming sword, from Assyria. Why in writing and why at that time rather than at another? The two kingdoms, Judah and Israel, had been separated only a short time, and yet their characters were already strongly differentiated. In the kingdom of Judah, that is, in Jerusalem, under the reign of Asa, the venerable wooden Ark of the nomads had, since Solomon's time, been enclosed in a stone temple, where it would remain, and whence it rendered its oracles. That the temple was an annex of the king's palace reminds us that Yahweh was a simple national god, tied to a people, tied to a land, as were Baal or Moloch. Like all patriots, Yahweh became jealous, suspicious, biased, vindictive, violent: in short, a god like the others, a god devoid of interest. To simplify and caricature matters, things were not the same in the kingdom of Israel which, one might venture to say, had the luck not to have the relic or the remains of its national or nationalized deity confined in a specific spot; thus the cult there was non-centralized, more uniformly widespread; it was not tied to a determinate space, nor was it physically adjacent to the political power. This power itself, moreover, was at once shared and disputed between king and clergy on the one hand, and the Prophets on the other, that is to say men who, neither bound by a dogma nor restrained by a rite, moved about from village to village reminding the people of the ancient wisdom of the Patriarchs of the nomadic era and attesting that, according to the religion of their fathers, the heart of man is the sole temple where the Eternal dwells. Even if that god, too, finally came to be called Yahweh, it is, at the very least, forbidden to speak his name, and that is a victory of the Elohist tradition: the God of the ancestors, the God of Abraham and Jacob, the God of the nomads, is Elohim,[1] the universal divine principle who is linked neither to a people nor to a land, who is a god of time and not, as Yahweh will be, a god of space. Elohim is the true Jewish god.

The entire ideological history of the people of Israel can be presented as dominated by this conflict between Elohim and Yahweh,[2] between the nomadic and the sedentary life, between the thought of time and the thought of space, between internal morality represented by time, nomadism, fidelity, and external power represented by space, sedentarization, the State. At the time of the Patriarchs there was, by definition, no problem: it was Elohism that reigned: God was in man's heart. The interior space of the Ark, that portable place where the Law (Torah) is deposited, is designated by the same word (*kerev*) used to name the internal space of the human body, that pulmonary, abdominal, vaginal, uterine cavity, the pregnant womb, which each person conveys everywhere with him or herself.[3] Always identical, but never in the same spot. Time is the great law of nomadic life: it serves to measure space, in hours or days of walking; it serves to set rendezvous, and it is noteworthy that the religion of the Patriarchs is a religion whose major festivals, like its encounters, are in time, not in space. Time has left its living mark on the whole Jewish religion.

The certainty that Elohim exists, that the world is not an immense blind machine that crushes human beings, the absolute confidence in the divine promise, the loving contemplation of the creator, the exclusive preoccupation with purity of heart, all that both differentiates Hebraic culture from those cultures which surround it geographically, and does not predispose the soul, dazzled by the single God, to concern itself with worldly affairs. Thus a place is left empty, which Yahweh will try to fill.

After centuries of wandering life, which began with the departure from Chaldea at the beginning of the second millennium, until post-Mosaic sedentarization, six or seven hundred years later, when the Hebrews settled in one location, there was not simply a replacement of nomadic ideology by sedentary ideology. There were mixtures, superimpositions and conflicts, some of which still endure in Judaism. A victory of the Elohists (or a collective remorse) revoked the right to speak the name of Yahweh; a victory of the Yahwists kept Yahweh as the name of God. A victory of the Elohist spirit allowed the omnipresence of the divine and of joy to be the very fabric of the Jewish religion; a victory of Yahwist thought allowed Solomon to erect the temple and to entrust it to specialized priests. And what of the remorse which, in the form of the eye of God, pursued Cain, the sedentary farmer, who had killed his nomadic brother Abel, the shepherd? A victory of the Elohist spirit made music, poetry, dance, in short the arts of time, the preferred expressions of Jewish culture; a more qualified success of the Yahwist spirit organized a temple around the Ark in Jerusalem, a rare—if not the sole—example of architecture of the people of Israel; yet the materials for this temple, such as cedar, came from Tyre; this was probably true of the architects as well. If there is a plastic art, it is always as a consequence, so to speak, of a consideration of time.

This is true of cult objects, which are relatively rare and always portable. Even the *urim* and *thummim* which permitted the rendering of oracles in high antiquity were not a tripod installed—as in Delphi—in the crevice of a rock communicating, in a specific spot, with the bowels of the earth, but a sort of lottery wheel that the priests wore around their necks in a breastplate. The Hannukah lamp is the materialization of a length of time: a week. As for books, if they are the spatialization of a thought, at least they are to be read in time and to be carried. Religious punctiliousness even went so far as to forbid that the Torah touch the ground, the most terrible denial that the nomadic imperative was able to inflict on the sedentary temptation, a denial still in force. And if there is a design, let it be in the book, readable and portable just as it is; in short, a miniature, an illumination, an embellishment of the letter, often devised, moreover, as a commentary.

The two great monotheisms of the Middle East, Judaism and Islam, still reveal their link to nomadic life in that their founding monument is a book, a portable object, and that they repudiate idols, those untransportable statues which constitute the mythological arsenal of polytheistic empires. Writing constitutes, on the contrary, their sole possible monument, because it is the most condensed means of reproducing the real, the medium closest to immaterial thought: writing is already the model, the reduction of space, its opening on a discourse, on the duration of a reading and on the internalization of performances. That entire peoples know how to read, in a world which restricted reading and writing strictly to castes of scribes, is yet another paradox of nomadism; but the sacred text cannot take root, and if it must always be carried, that is because the divine word has no native soil. It reigns over the whole universe.

To dream of space, of the domination of space, is to dream of grandeur, to compete with the Eternal. To construct a tower so high it equals or surpasses Him. To construct a state whose sovereignty rivals His. Babel or Babylon, it is the same word. The dream of establishing itself in space has certainly always haunted the Jewish soul; it tried many times to do so and each time found itself in a position where it had either to fail or to abandon its very Jewishness.[4] The fact remains that the message persistently addressed to the Gentiles is that such a dream is senseless for, even when it succeeds, it is at far too high a price: the renunciation of justice, love, inner life and peace of body, mind, soul and heart. There is only one thing the demon, if he exists, has ever been able to offer man to disgrace him: power.

What power? I can give myself the illusion that I am master of space, because I can move in it and then retrace my steps. That is not true of time which promises everything but also outmodes everything, including spatial wandering. Time does not permit error, return, erasure or approximation; it is irreversibility itself. Thence the unique, anguished, solemn character of prophetism, of messianism, of the realization of the city of God, of all the great encounters with history that constitute the framework of Jewish thought. The tree of Boaz itself which, as a tree, symbolizes power and promise, is only the statement of a genealogy formulated prior to its realization, as other lineages are formulated in the Bible, interminably, after the fact. What is important is that time is an implacable and unique order, in which the Eternal, that is He who is in possession of all His time—and ours—effects the inevitable and permits all certainties for, if the order of time is irreversible, it is, by the same token, stable; it is the sole reality on which one can count. The flashback does not exist in reality: one can return to the past only by narrative or by phantasm; except by a special nominal decree of

the Eternal. It is said that Joshua was the bene-
ficiary of such an arrangement which allowed him
provisionally to stop the passing of time; or Boaz,
to whom God lent new youthfulness in order to
accomplish His broad design; but the law is that
one cannot grow younger, and that one can get
around the idea of death only by a verbal, futile
and derisory trick. That is what makes Victor
Hugo's quatrain so irresistibly poignant:

> It is long since she who shared my bed
> Left it for yours, Oh Lord;
> And yet still we are mingled one with the other
> She half alive and I half dead.

Jewish anguish and pessimism spring ultimately from this intuition of time which does not
appear at all in the same forms or with the same
content in the other religions and mythologies of
antiquity. Everything happens in the Bible as
though the preoccupation with space, the first
concern of those who construct cities, had not
yet replaced the nomads' obsession with time.

Of course, the history of the people of Israel
is not composed of decisive success or of the
temporal or spatial principle: it is made up of
contradictory juxtapositions, of compromises, or
else regrets which are more or less repressed and
ready to rise again. Those whose enthusiasm runs
to conflicts, transcendencies or syntheses risk
being disappointed here. For there are contradic-

tions that remain and which, so to speak, coexist, neither unnoticed nor resolved, sometimes throughout millennia.[5] Or else the contradictions are acknowledged in a movement which denies both at one and the same time. The major artfulness—not to say astuteness—of Jewish thought has been, on this very point, to approach everything by writing, above all else, by the names of things. Better yet: by the initial of that name, that is to say by the symbol of the beginning. For if the history of Israel is holy, it is because all history is holy, because history is the cult of time. As for language, it is holy and primordial; it, too, is initial since, as soon as God had created things, He presented them to the first man to name. Thus, things have the same age as their name and saying their initial is, in a manner of speaking, telling all about them, to the point where the relationship between a name and a thing becomes the relationship between the word and its initial.[6]

We know the importance of the first word of Genesis: *bereshit*. It begins with the second letter of the alphabet. We can then suppose that there exists an *aleph*, a prebeginning, but of which nothing can be said. As for the first word itself, generally translated as "in the beginning," it gives a signal. A double signal: on the one hand, the starting signal of the text of the Torah which tradition holds to be, from its first to its last letter, the very name of the Eternal, so that reading the Torah from one end to the other would be, all things considered, merely naming God: Being always rediscovered in discourse and discourse in being.[7]

But, on the other hand, *bereshit* sends out a still more important signal, that of a thought for which the narrative "from the outset" is the first and perhaps the final step of intellection for, if things are history, telling their history is obviously the only way to understand them.

Consider, for instance, two possible attitudes toward history, toward the narrative *ab initio*. At the end of the nineteenth century, psychology operated by means of great concepts, such as those of perception, memory, imagination, affectivity, and so forth. There was an attempt to reconcile them with reality by means of clinical examples, pertinent observations, but it was known, too, that this psychology, however concrete it might wish to be, stopped at the threshold of the individual because he was formed by a series of singular past events and, in order to know him, it would be necessary to reconstruct his individual history. This was a strange fear to have impeded this young science and a strange renunciation of the very program which stated the way out of the impasse. On the whole, all Sigmund Freud did (because he was steeped in Jewish thought?) was to prescribe as the method of the science the very history which had been claimed to stand in its way.[8] Was it necessary to work up the history of the individual? Very well, let's tackle the *bereshit* at the outset or, as is said in jest: Tell me about your early childhood.

You, too, tell me about your early childhood, or let me tell about it in my own way, you whom my primary school teachers represented to me as hirsute patriarchs "dressed in animal skins" or else "in candid probity and white linen"; you who are, too, thanks to the nerve-wracking play of cultures, my early childhood, whether I like it or not, as well as the childhood of some billions of other men; you about whom all I know, finally, is that you wrote a book about which I do not know very much. And worst of all is that in making your Elohim the God of time, you knew for a fact, it is clearly spelled out, that generations and the famous "world without end" would share your obsession with time, your anxiety about the future and vertigo of the past when we look back at you driving your meager livestock over those dunes that we have stripped to extract their pestilential oil. For we are your future: the future is today. Will there be a future of the future? Some of our prophets, who speak in megatons of I know not what, have calculated that there will not be, which is rather reassuring, for those prophets have always been mistaken.

And what means have we at our disposal for

this narrative? Slight, scarcely legible traces, letters, initials of words or initials of syllables, as there are no vowels. Certainly all of that has been edited and re-edited hundreds of times, translated and retranslated into all languages and annotated interminably. Everyone found "lessons" in it: those they were looking for of course. Now, it is our turn. The biblical myth is rich enough so that, if shaken up a bit, it helps tell what world we want, and how it may be approached.

* * *

There are two principal lessons of Judaism: the first is the unconditional character of the exigency of justice and the second the inwardness of the moral law. One can grasp Jewish thought only if one sees clearly and concretely what these two messages contest.

The first is, strictly speaking, revolutionary, because it gives priority to what must *be* over what *is*, because it implies turning reality inside out, and already begins to accomplish this by turning its attention and its heart toward those who are forgotten and scorned, the poor, the oppressed, the *anavim*, the humble friends of God. In the ancient pagan world, this Jewish lesson is scandalous, it is scandal itself, because it attacks the most profound structures of societies and empires. Is it really otherwise today?

The second message denies that true piety

consists in religious acts and demands something infinitely more difficult: inner conversion, close adherence of the soul to virtue. This second precept is obviously interdependent with the first; it is, as it were, both the consequence and the condition, in the psychological order, of the will to justice in the social order.

Let us note this carefully: Western anti-Semitism, in rejecting the Jew as "different," perceived at the same time the nomadic character of Judaism and its indifference, indeed even its hostility, to nations and to states. This gave rise to the stereotyped figure of the wandering and stateless Jew. Why has this figure been useful for transmitting racist prejudices from generation to generation? For one thing, it is possible, if not probable, that peoples linked by natural or social necessity to a specific native soil saw in the Jew, as in the Gypsy or other nomads, the realization of a liberty which was inaccessible to them and whose temptation had to be exorcized by the hasty fabrication of some protective armor, of some loud and clear proclamation of the virtue of native soils, homes and homelands. But, on the other hand, by one of those breathtaking paradoxes of which Christian thought has the secret, anti-Semitism will reproach the Jews, the race most attached to their culture and their law, with not having ties, meaning, here, spatial ties. Why this particular restriction to roots in one locality? Is it not, first of all, the refusal to recognize the moral rather than spatial character of the law, the absolute priority of the inwardness of the will over the display of institutions and their monuments?

It is probable that one of the components of anti-Semitism is the obstinate refusal of that universal law—which is, indeed, of Jewish origin and which is nothing but the moral law. The ambiguous attitude of Christian civilization toward Judaism and, more concretely, to Jews, is simply the duality of the acceptance and the rejection of morality, transposed into love or hatred of persons who are, for reasons which are difficult to understand, and contrary to all historical, sociological or demographic sense, set up as witnesses of the 3000-year-old Jewish proclamation according to which the world needs social justice and consequently purity of heart.

In order at last to have nothing further to do with this law or, if you will, in order no longer to find themselves confronting the law and its sole author alone, Christian eras fearfully invented hundreds of intercessions, from the group of saints under Mary's glory to the Roman Catholic materiality of a hierarchy of the clergy; ranging from the tripartition of the divinity on the theoretical level to the idolatry of statues and icons on the practical level. This pagan paraphernalia, despite certain countermeasures such as the different attempts at reform, has the intolerable advantage of presenting the world to the believer as though it were acceptable in its actual form, peopled as it would be by manifestations of holiness, capable of counterbalancing the forces of evil. Whence the occasional hysterical outburst of fascination with fiction and feelings whose most accomplished form, scarcely attained by ancient paganism even in its Dionysian festivals, is baroque art.

In the face of these excesses, Jewish thought can seem to be, and to some degree admit to being, schizoid, that is, etymologically, cut off from the world, taking on a posture of denial, of retreat; and this retreat, as we know, is first of all retreat toward the book.

* * *

The biblical vision of history offers great originality and somewhat upsets the representations authorized by scientific or positivist thought. For example, for the Bible (and here it is tempting to add: for all Jewish thought), the end of a process is already contained in the process itself, and this process is somehow contained in its beginning, in its initial. One thinks of the Prophets, for whom the end of history, paradise regained and the eternal kingdom of justice, are present within today's crimes and these crimes, in turn, in the origin of the world, so that the divine will, the absolute good, is the real content of the evil of which man is guilty. The outcome is integral to history itself. Here is an indication that if Jewish discourse is a narrative, a chronicle involving primarily a chronology, this narrative is not the narration of just anything. Events occur, they do not bring themselves about. The world is not chance, because God is not caprice, and the chronology is not a simple succession, it is order, which dates the moments of the world. The Lord embarked us with Him on an adventure which, after all, is His. We did not appear by chance, we are at the very least a necessary moment. A moment of what? Necessary to what? But what did that literate nomad, whose very dust has now disappeared, mean, 3000 years ago, when he took seriously his absurd dream of a God who realizes that He now must create man? Could not that God, if I might so put it, get Himself out of it all alone? Is the answer to Job's questions: yes, it is "pleasure to the Almighty that thou art righteous," it is "gain to him that thou makest thy ways perfect" (Job 22:3)? But then, if that is the case, we will have to leave our goods spread out in space, divest ourselves of our superhighways and freezers, think about time and about the future, in short, become in our hearts the nomads of Elohim, wherever that may lead us.

To do so, one must first renounce empires, renounce power. According to a cabalistic reading, human thought can be defined, in a first approximation, on three levels, which are, from the highest to the lowest: *mohar*, literally, "the white of the brain," the abstract moment of thought; then *lev*, the heart, the intermediate stage; and finally *kaved*, "the liver" (literally, "the heavy"), the most formed, most concrete state of thought. The process is analagous to that of digestion and refers to an internal anatomical space, not to a geographical space. The king is charged by God with effecting in the city the thought process which goes from *mohar*, the thought of the law, to *kaved*, its concrete formation, in passing through *lev*, the heart. It is therefore inevitable that the political function be named, using the initials of these three elements: m, l, k, *melek*, "the king," literally—that is, letter by letter—he who gives form to thought (of God). This king will never, in fact, be a king in the Western sense; Judaism has always been incapable of creating a State like the great Eastern or Hellenic Empires: the "king" is at least equally a great priest, his mission is related more to God than to man. He is there not to set armies into motion, but rather to lead men back to justice, and the Prophets remind him of that if he forgets. All his attempts to make himself powerful in terms of space risk making him unfaithful in terms of time. When he tries to turn himself into the State, that is, make himself unjust and violent, he deJudaizes himself. In short: he draws away from Elohim.

* * *

The peoples who experienced a diaspora, sometimes repeatedly in the course of their history and prehistory, are innumerable. If we grant the fact that the human race, which today occupies the entirety of the land masses, originally appeared in only two or three places, it is obvious that all peoples experienced the diaspora. Now, what is the great law of the diaspora? The fact that it results in acculturation. The Magyars no longer show any evidence of their past history in the north of present-day Russia, nor do the Greeks of the time when they had not even seen the sea, nor the Indians of the three Americas of the time when, according to Paul Rivet, having come from Southeast Asia, they made the circuit of the Pacific Ocean. The present-day nations, anchored to a soil, differentiated by language and culture, each represent both a particular characteristic mode of acculturation to new conditions of life and the collective loss of memory of their origins despite, or thanks to, legends. But these real origins are, always, extraterritorial.

Yet, this law is false as far as the Jews are

concerned. To the point where the very word *diaspora* seems reserved to their diaspora. It is as though the people of Israel, demographically augmented by all those who adhere to their religion, found its unity and identity negatively in dispersion, while other peoples lived this diaspora as an element of division and as an irresistible factor of diversification. Why?

Perhaps the Babylonian captivity furnishes the symbolic explanation of this phenomenon. A conquered and captive people, in part reduced to slavery, and whose religious symbols are destroyed, a people who have lost their kings, in short, a people whom God seems to have abandoned, resists for fifty years, and even goes further than that, turning this ordeal to account by rediscovering a unity it could not maintain in days of prosperity and liberty. Why? Only one response is possible here. It is that the Hebraic culture of the time was *entirely*, and of course unwittingly, geared toward the confrontation of such an historical situation, perhaps because it sprang from such a confrontation, eleven centuries earlier during the sojourn in Egypt. This culture, broadly definable as nomadic culture, shows two characteristics which not only resist the diaspora, but also find in it a source of nourishment and strength, along with the consciousness of a unity and a particular mission. In the first place, the fundamental elements of this culture are mobile, portable; one always takes them along, wherever one might go. First and foremost, it is the heart of man that is the dwelling place of Elohim. Then, the Ark has two shafts like a sedan chair. Finally, the ensemble of all the implements of the cult—practical proofs of the unity of the community—is conceived as traveling equipment.

Then, and despite some stray impulses toward spatial power, the fact remains that this culture's vision of itself and of the people it affects is a thoroughly temporal vision, where the essential is the past beginning with the creation and the future until its fulfillment. God is a god who endures, perhaps He is duration itself; whereas the other great gods of antiquity, in this same region of the world, are gods of space, linked to a land, and are explicitly situated outside of time.

Only radically atheistic ages can thoroughly understand what constitutes not the privilege but the originality of Jewish culture. If only they do not miss its poetry!

It would here be indispensable to know the situation, on these general points, of the peoples who are still in (or have returned to) a nomadic or seminomadic state; those peoples whom all states persecute or, if you will, whom capital has not succeeded in sedentarizing in order to chain them to production.

As for the Hebrews, they did more than withstand each diaspora, they nurtured themselves from it because, unlike other peoples, they had kept their nomadic culture, or something of their nomadic culture. Insofar as each sedentarization is built on regret for nomadic thought and remorse for having abandoned it (regret and remorse are, moreover, sentiments which concern time), each diaspora, on the contrary, while it denotes a misfortune or a (spatial) uprooting, also brings a (temporal) gain, a reacquisition and a reconciliation. Nomadic culture is preserved all the more as it has never been entirely lost and as there is joy in recovering it. But, once again, why the Hebrews rather than any other human group?

All that is disturbing indeed. The origin of the Hebrews, like that of all small tribes of high antiquity, is not really known or understood. It is not even known if there is a connection between their name and the Arab *Ibrim*, "those from the other side" (of the river?) or the old Egyptian *Habirou*, "those who come from the desert." In the course of time, they, like all peoples, forged a national religion, which soon came into conflict with neighboring religions. But on the other hand, with this people, who were late to settle in a fixed area and who were ceaselessly torn by internal wars which weakened them further with respect to external powers, nothing happens as it does with other peoples.

59

Nothing happens as it does with other peoples. What will subsequently become of Judaism? In the Diaspora, what will remain of the Hebraic heritage and, revived and reactivated, enriched, too, by every actual situation lived by Jews in the course of history, will constitute Jewish thought and culture?

All Jewish communities, said to be more easily identified as such during ages of religious faith, persist despite persecutions from without and probably, in part, because of them. But only in part. The perpetuity of the community is linked principally to internal positive factors, for Jewish culture is fundamentally turned toward values, ways of life and of feeling which specifically give priority to continuity above all else. Is not the only absolute imperative of the Jewish religion, and of Jewish ethics as well, to "perpetuate Israel?"

It is noteworthy that this thought of time which, to a certain extent, excludes the thought of space, became practically a permanent characteristic of Jewish culture, influencing even its esthetic sensibility. As Bruno Zevi points out,[9] if there are innumerable Jewish writers, poets and musicians, there is not one great Jewish architect. Even Solomon had to send to Tyre for the builders of the Temple. This is not true with respect to painting; remember, however, that Soutine arrived in Paris a cripple, the victim of his schoolmates who threw stones at him when they saw him painting a portrait of the rabbi.

During an era when, in a country like France, regionalist claims and differentiations are again being asserted, at a moment when several cultures seek themselves through or behind a veneer of so-called centralizing and "Jacobinism" (although it goes back at least as far as the time of Louis XIV), it is surprising to ascertain that the majority of local cultures—Basque, Picard, Breton or Savoyard—seem to have been surprised, as it were, by the centralism of the nation-state. They found out they were mortal only when already moribund. If they wish to survive, they must adapt themselves to the struggle for survival, they must furnish themselves with means of endurance: accordingly, they will immediately seek the first of these means in writing, in books. Jewish civilization has already done so; it has always been made for survival. If it, too, needs to be reawakened, renewed, Jewish civilization has only to express itself to collect itself, to get its bearings, even if the civilization recovers itself only to wonder on what basis it does so.

Another rather permanent dimension of Jewish thought, and probably the most important one for Western societies, is its incomparable critical power. If there is a common characteristic of ways of thinking as different as those of Spinoza, Marx, Freud, Schönberg, Kafka and Einstein, it is perhaps that they all cast a questioning and skeptical glance at the object of their reflection, at the very basis of generally accepted ideas concerning that object. It is clear that these thinkers were—to different degrees—integrated into the societies in which they lived: without his having read Descartes, there would have been no Spinoza; without the medical education of Vienna, Nancy or the Salpêtrière, no Freud; without the tonal tradition of Western music, no Schönberg; without Prague, no Kafka. But, still, these authors, although they understood and assimilated the surrounding culture, were not, for all that, assimilated to it; thanks, probably, to their Jewish moral and psychological background, they were able to integrate this culture without being integrated into it, take it without being taken in by it. Perhaps they always somewhat distrusted it, despite whatever admiration it inspired in them. It is tempting to explain this situation by the general rejection of Judaism: the challenged turns challenger. Here, again, such an explanation is partially true, if everything is taken into account, but insufficient in the aggregate. It takes no effort to enter into Jewish culture in order to find what predisposes it, internally, to such critical efficacy.

In order to reply to such a question, it is necessary (I was about to say: as always) to return to the Prophets. They did not allow themselves to be taken in by the world, either; they, too, had this internal and external critical attitude which makes their observations caustic and irrefutable. Why? Because they had both an absolute and a relative postulate at their mental command, a term beyond history and reality, that is, divine will and the promise of a world of justice in an indefinite but certain future; and a term immersed in history and in time, that is, reality as it manifested itself to them. The mental mechanism by which prophetism breaks away from the actual world is analogous to that which, ever since Genesis, made time the first dimension of the act of creation and of its realized creatures; for if time is everything, everything in it is situated, relative, nothing is eternal, nothing is given as is in an unambiguous, necessary and immutable manner. God Himself made the world in six days, and then He rested. Six days, for Him whose power is limitless? Rested, He who should be capable of everything, at once? Yes. Let us not form too high an idea of God; He was, after all, only created by man. However, man gave Him, God, the most important, if not the best, aspect of his own human existence: his inexorable submission to the law of time and, consequently, the relativity of his works.

Only the misguided, whom the prophet chastises and wants to lead back to the truth, can believe that what is can become the standard of what will be or of what used to be. Jewish thought is thus constituted and reinforced around two terms, one of which, in truth, is always missing: that is God, or the absolute, or the Messiah, or justice realized. The other term, which is the actual given, is completely relative, made completely relative by the first and, so to speak, returned to its proper place. The absolute functions as a relativizing factor of the other term, even if it is nothing in itself, even if it is nothingness. In short, critical relativism, even if it considers itself formulated on an absolute, in reality only asserts the negation of the given and the possibility of becoming detached from it. Solely on account of the encompassing ideology does it consider itself obliged to disguise its character of negation behind a supposed metaphysical or theological positivity.

The characteristic by which Jewish thought is infallibly recognized is that it immediately grasps every object as non-obligatory and inconclusive in itself, as an object whose worth is set by its counterpoint, even in cases where its counterpoint is nothing. Non-Jewish consciousness falls into the trap of believing in things as they seem to be, always with some small aspect of the absolute, a gloss of eternity or of necessity, of universal truth. It too often lacks that irreplaceable sense of the relativity of things which total immersion in temporality lends to thought.

It is clear that these affirmations themselves must be taken as partial approximations. First because numerous individuals of Jewish culture might, for diverse reasons, not have retained this aspect of the mental universe in which they matured. Or the reverse. Then because Judaism, particularly because of its propensity toward universality, has, so to speak, made—or tried to make—a gift of this form of thought to the West: that is perhaps what is meant by that strange hybrid known as *Judeo-Christian* civilization. With the result that countless osmoses, countless crossbreedings and those infinite internal currents that surreptitiously traverse societies and their discourses, their knowledge, their practices and their imaginations, sometimes engender the most unexpected and yet the most obvious figures. Nothing is simple. Fortunately: otherwise, if all were uniform, one could not get one's bearings.

* * *

It remains to be seen, or at least to wonder, if the originality of the Hebrews who, in the midst of a universe of great "eternal" empires, were never completely sedentarized, results from a real difference in their life, their mores and their social practices vis-à-vis neighboring peoples. Is it true that nothing happens with them as it does with other peoples or is it only that the Bible made us believe that? If so, it would be as notable a peculiarity as real, deep-seated differences. Limit-less power of the written text, in antiquity: history narrated, retrievable, repeatable, verifiable. The written word has not, as it has for us, lost all credibility; it is, on the contrary, the basis of certainties, something like evidence. At the moment the legend becomes a written thing, it acquires the force of law, lays the foundation of a culture, if not, indeed, of a State: it becomes a reference and thus is transformed from the dream it was into truth.

One summer day, in Ithaca, a sailor refused, under the pretext of a storm, to take me out in a boat; in fact, there were only a few centimeters of choppy waves in the sea. I thought of Ulysses and his sailors, whose imagination had perhaps multipled ten- or a hundredfold the height of the waves and transformed a light wind into a hurricane. It is, certainly, hard to bring one's boat back to port in foul weather. But is it not a hundred times more astonishing to contrive, with language alone, that we still, after twenty or thirty centuries, talk about a voyage which, if it took place at all, was only perhaps a paltry outing? What counts is that since certain words have had a certain set order, any daring, long or complicated voyage is an "odyssey" and any adventure "Homeric." Perhaps with the Bible, then, the Hebrews, in their own way, effected a process similar to that of the Greek epic, but one much more important to Western history. By the power and prestige of the word, by the evidential nature of the written word, a legend is transformed into history, a lie into truth, a dream into exigency. That being so, the most insignificant anecdote can become, according to the way it is narrated and the strength of feeling attached to it, the center of thought and action for billions of men; this is undoubtedly the case with the lives of the Patriarchs, and of episodes so rich in meaning for us, such as the story of the golden calf or of the judgment of Solomon. Strange, disturbing, fascinating power of the word and of the written word: the power of letters, the miracle of alphabets.

But let there be no mistake. The written word, even if it is the power of falsehood, is, above all, in the use the Hebrews make of it, the effective power of negation, of denial. To affirm the City of God, to write and describe the reign of justice, is certainly a falsehood, because that reign and that city are illusory, because the world is full of injustice and impiety. But this is done essentially in order to oppose to this unjust world a radical, absolute, unconditional refusal, a refusal which appears in its most pathetic form in Job and in Amos: if the world cannot be just, then let it vanish. A refusal which, in countless varied forms, from Jeremiah to Marx and from the *anavim* to Marcuse, constitutes the rallying point of all who maintain an ideal, a hope, and who, as a result, are thereby attached, whether or not they want to be, whether or not they know it, to Israelite thought.

That thought, that writing, is the only one of those which come to us from the past which is uncontestably seditious, that is, which is the first recourse of the imaginary against the real, a protest against the established order, and even society's cry of revolt against the State,[10] the cry of life against oppression. Consequently, writing, from its beginning, is in league with art which, if only as a "souvenir of accumulated suffering,"[11] is also a cry of revolt or, at the very least, of refusal.

If this is indeed the most important dimension of the Bible, it goes without saying that successive generations have tried to cover up this message, to mask it. It also goes without saying that none has entirely succeeded. Thus, the ideological function of reference to the Bible in the revolts of the Middle Ages, including the peasant revolts, is explained:

> When Adam delved and Eve span
> Who was then the gentleman?

Christianity on high, adroit at using one of God's orders to justify the successive submissions of the slave to the master, of the serf to the noble, of the proletarian to the employer, would never have lasted socially and historically if there had not been a Christianity below leaving biblical purity to express the dreams of the lower classes.

Revolt. Refusal. Are we warranted in giving thought to Abraham, born in Ur, but who, as is said, leaves Chaldea to go off wandering toward Canaan on God's order? He is the sedentary man who becomes a nomad, the man of the city who leaves it for the wide open spaces. Why? To escape what Brecht will call the Jungle of Cities, to be no longer an extra cog in the machine, in short to say *no* and by this very movement to set himself up and affirm himself in his subjectivity. That is what it is to be a man: to refuse. The animal, the slave, the senseless ones accept, continue, reproduce. They have no inwardness, *that is to say no place of refusal*, of negation, of criticism. Nor any foundation for that refusal which finally springs forth, always in the name of a subjective preference or impossibility or desire. Abraham, whose final name comprises the same consonants as the name of the Hebrews, is probably the first free man of biblical antiquity,[12] because he is the first to say no to the world and therefore yes to God, because he would have gone so far as to sacrifice his son to Him. Totally calm, Abraham leaves a city situated at a precise point in space, he leaves places like his native land, his home, as well as everything attached to it, to go to live thenceforth where the Eternal leads him; he does not abandon himself, he entrusts himself to absolute difference, to the succession where all becomes possible. In short, he leaves space for time, that is to say slavery for liberty. This tenth generation descendent of Shem was rightly recognized as the father of the Jews, and of all free men.

For liberty is the true wandering, the true nomadism: it neither knows where it is going nor can it have a model. To prescribe an aim, an objective for it is, derisively, to annihilate it. Engels' theme of liberty as "understood necessity," endlessly harped on by all Stalinists, only leads to dictatorships. It would be Abraham renouncing the desert; it is Babylon; it is captivity. Free men, like nomads, are those who do not know where they are going.[13]

Moreover, on the theoretical level, prescribing an aim for liberty, telling it at the outset where it will end up, is the same as distrusting time, not really believing in its creative powers. Unless, worse yet, it is an attempt to dominate time, to exercise power over it. Which God Himself does not seem to dare! He who says where liberty is going, where it must go, sets himself up as stronger than the Creator. He has broken the contract. It is he whom time will engulf.

This poses the urgent question of fundamental values, treated by all philosophers since

Nietzsche. Is it better to be free? Obligatory to be just? And if there is an alternative between God and Satan, why not choose the latter?

As everyone knows, one must, to be in fashion, opt for objective necessities and opt against liberty, for cynicism and against justice, for Satan and against God. If, on the other hand, one has read the Torah as an apologia for good, one will virtuously choose the other response.

But, to parry a question with a question, is that really an alternative, either God or Satan? Is not liberty, the condition of possibility of choice, necessary for this alternative to exist?

Liberty, that is, the *presence of the negative*. If the world is complete, Abraham has but to stay in Ur; moreover, nowhere can he find the reasons or the will or the means to leave it. He is no longer Abraham.

This perhaps clears up our initial query and, in a sense, turns it inside out. Judaism has undeniably retained the proud memory of its nomadic times. But we must not believe that this nostalgia concerns some primeval, primordial, given moment; it is not a collective form of Oedipus. For the nomadic era itself—its purity, its simplicity, its liberty—far from being a natural state, is already a *conquest*, a precious good which was seized, which cost Abraham the first step away from the *Ibrim*, from the other side of the river. What is given and primordial is the repetition, the captivity in the determinisms of the world; it is Ur, it is slavery: the former is forgotten. What is won is nomadic life, free and unforgettable life. Francis Picabia, only one of the innumerable fighters for the right of refusal and of rejection, said that "it is necessary to be a nomad, to traverse ideas as one traverses countries and cities." It is comprehensible that the sedentary resettlement at the time of the Kings revived the Hebrews' memory of the time of the Patriarchs and of libertarian nomadism. It gave rise to all the spiritual adventures, in the first rank of which was that paradoxical but stubborn love of justice, that absolute priority given to subjectivity despite appearances accounting it powerless. The Jewish soul understood, dimly at first and then, at the time of the Prophets, with anguish, that the State was the worst danger, the most perverse temptation. Whatever it might be, wherever it might be, it reduces everything again to the level of the brute beast. It was Einstein who noted the uselessness of a brain in those who submit to power, noting bitterly "the spinal cord would have been enough." It was Isaac Bashevis Singer who pointed out, in Paris, in December 1978, that the Yiddish language had never served to pronounce a death sentence and that one cannot say, in Yiddish, *attention*! Probably the most important message that Judaism has to bring to our time, and the most tragic explanation of the persecutions to which it is subjected, is that a culture—or cultures—need not be state controlled, or linked to a power.

Some will read the Bible as the actual, literal statement of the divine commandments. Others as an ethnological document. Still others as a poem, or a nightmare, or a medley of sparse and essentially insignificant texts.

For me, there is in fact a good bit of "jamming" in the text, interferences among ideology, form, language, truth. But the truth can still be discerned, as social complexity has not yet made the "jamming" impenetrable. The aspect of the Bible that has resisted not only the sands but the even more corrosive workings of the scribes, scholars and clergy is the visible trace of the conflict between the city and the desert, between servitude and refusal, between a world of entirely given objects and a minority of potentially rebellious subjects. Nothing more. The Bible is neither the certainty of love nor the evidence of hope. It is only their possibility and the mathematically infinitesimal chance of a different course of time. It is only a spark in the midst of eternal night, but that spark is everything.

* * *

"Time is money" is probably the preeminent capitalist expression and one of the most glaring absurdities that has ever been thought of. Only the system of wage-earning has in fact succeeded in exchanging for money the days of a life, that is fragments of the human being himself, because his life is, in the final analysis, a succession of days, of hours and of minutes which the wage-earner retails individually. Statisticians use the hour as the unit of work. On the whole, time lived is a commodity which is traded, retailed and, since manpower or labor reserves exist, even stockpiled. Of course, the fact that salary buys time is concealed by ideology: it is said, for example, that the worker earns his living whereas in reality he loses his life.

In the Bible, it is exactly the reverse. Time is not a commodity: it is a gift. It is not exchanged, it elapses and in passing is replaced by nothing. Time is a permanent substitution without a substitute. "In place" of the vanished instant, there is nothing, there is nothingness; as a matter of fact, there is no "place." And death, that term of individual time, is non-substitution as well. It is not the passage to another life; in the *sheol*, in the tomb, one no longer has feeling, or desire, or memory, or perception. Death can be spoken of only in the negative.

But if time is a gift, it is one which is limited and non-renewable. The duration of the world is finite, even if it is incomparably longer than human life. Everything happens as though the existence of the universe, too, had a duration, whose beginning we know from Genesis and whose end we know will be total presence or the "end of time," which comes to the same thing since time is a system of absences.

The lengths of human lives are posited within this great cosmic duration and can even be used to measure it roughly; thus, one often counts in "generations."

In the Bible, there is a whole series of techniques of time, which deserve detailed study, and which all revolve around what is perhaps the major problem of those who have nothing but time (those who do not possess objects firmly secured in space): it is necessary that they fix their guideposts in time, and yet nothing is fixed in time where there can be no stationary landmarks. That is the insoluble paradox of nomadism and of liberty.

All peoples have based a calendar on cosmic movements, particularly those of the Sun and the Moon. Whatever it may be, this calendar is, in the final analysis, only the spatialization of time, because a date is the moment when a certain star is in a certain spot in the sky, in relation to fixed landmarks on earth. Man has always measured time by space, whether it be by the movement of a heavenly body, or that of a hand on the face of a clock. This contrivance might well be strongly symbolic. For, after all, why measure time? To dominate it? A senseless pretension. To stop it?

Madness. To sell it? Perfidy. To tell it? Well and good, but then a rough measure is sufficient. Therefore, the Bible and all of Jewish life are merely made rhythmic.

On the one hand, of course, as in all mythologies, there are celebrations of past events, which are, moreover, linked to the solstices and equinoxes. The flight from Egypt, the Babylonian captivity, the sacrifice of the Maccabees, so many anniversaries.

But, on the other hand, there is the specifically Jewish and seemingly indomitable phenomenon of the sabbath, *shabbes*, Saturday. Not that there is no social rhythm of work and rest outside Judaism and its influence on Christianities. What is important here is the empirical and concrete content that Judaism puts into *shabbes*, for it is that which really reveals the concept of time.

Of course, it is not immaterial that *shabbes* is established in the very image of the time that the Creator took to make the world. It is conclusive that He, whom nothing should tire if He is omnipotent, even thought it necessary "to rest." But that is anthropomorphism. It is doubtless necessary to seek further, elsewhere.

What? In short, during six days, God was turned toward things, toward the world. He did not, if I might so put it, have time to devote to Himself. He is going to take the time; the seventh day is the time of inwardness. That is it: the

Jewish God is a subject. Not only has He whims, plans, desires, but He even asserts a claim—to Himself, naturally—to His rights, such as legitimate inwardness. I imagine that that day, for the first *shabbes*, in the glory of accomplishment and peace attained, God listened to music; first, because music is without external reference or meaning; then, because it is the sole, absolutely pure art of time. He listened to music. Or He created it, which for Him is perhaps the same thing. In that case, thanking Him for it every week would be the least one could do. Be that as it may, listen to music on Saturday. It does not matter whether you set your Saturday another day, or diffuse it all through the week. It is not a matter of a rite, it is a question of elementary respect, of simply listening (again a musical word) to our life, to our time. It is the only point on which one must never compromise or waver: the right to inwardness. The duty of inwardness.

Not long ago, certain philosophers, disgusted—with good reason—with the "bourgeois subject," the deceptive projection of the importance of society administered to serve or simply to preserve the individual; and disgusted, too, with the overrefined and vacuous romanticism of an ideology said to be human, but whose concrete reality is the killing of human beings in the four corners of the globe—these philosophers, claiming to be modern, proclaimed the death of the subject and the end of humanism, thus accomplishing the final murder that the dominant ideology itself dare not perpetrate. By disposing of the last rights of the subject in a world which repents of having given the subject too many as it is, one becomes not merely the accomplice but a constituent element of the system.

When the subject disappears, so does the claim. Then, the calm of well-conducted, docile factories, the peace of the fields and the tranquillity of model schools resemble those of cemeteries. And it is precisely because each human life is both limited and irreversible that it is necessary, at the cost of overthrowing structures of production and of oppression, "to give time to time," as an extraordinary Judeo-Spanish proverb puts it. To let the subject recover itself outside the world's tumult. To understand that time saved and inwardness are so closely linked that they are, in real life, as well as somewhere in theory, synonyms.

* * *

In short, what gives life its value is the evidence and the certainty of death, the only promise of which there is proof that it will be kept. The West thought of death either in Christian terms of survival and resurrection or in so-called "atheistic" terms, as did Heidegger, who went so far as to say "the finite and limited character of human existence is more important than that existence itself." It is exactly the opposite message that the Bible gives, and that Spinoza recapitulated: "Wisdom is meditation not on death but on life" (*Ethics* IV, proposition 67). This is a strange and significant contradiction in Jewish thought: on the one hand it is permeated by an inquiry on time, even by an obsession with temporality; on the other hand, and despite being the first philosophy of the subject, it seems unaware of the time of the subject; that is, its limit; that is, death.

There is another limit, a spatial limit which never interested the Hebrews: the sea. For a seafaring people, everything begins at its shore; for a nomadic people, everything ends at its edge. One can go no further, no further wandering is possible; at the threshold of death, no further dreaming is possible. Spinoza left the synagogue in vain, he took the precept along with him. In order to have an object, any thought of death must first transform death into an altered life, which the Bible effects only in very rare instances.

A vision of history for which the world goes collectively toward a distant but assured salvation is one thing. It is not in the least incompatible with a vision of the person for which the latter goes individually toward nothingness. The only problem to which the Bible attaches any importance is knowing whether that person was able to accomplish his fate, that is to say, in concrete terms, if he lived through three or four generations. If he did, death is not a scandal, it does not call for comment, it is a simple date. One does not deplore the fact that the earth ends at the seashore (Job 42:17).

But, reciprocally, what is intolerable to Jewish thought is the idea that a being can die before fulfilling his destiny; the dybbuk is the spirit of one who died "prematurely," and takes possession of a living person in order to try, as it were, to conclude his role, to round out his existence. It is not a ghost seeking vengeance or asserting its rights. It is a person making himself complete, fulfilling himself, wiping out the error or the horror of early death. A phantom is hostile, ill-disposed, frightening. The dybbuk is good, it returns in order to do good; if the community wants to get rid of it, as in Ansky's famous play, *The Dybbuk*, that is because it disturbs the social order. But, in doing so, it carries out the divine order. In this sense, which is the sense of truth, the dybbuk is an object of love. Love which is scandal and disgrace to partisans of order but certainty and happiness to those on the side of justice.

Here again—and nothing in antiquity could be more atheistic—"God needs man." He needs each man to go, in all senses of the word, to the end of his destiny, to neither recoil from it nor perish untimely.

As long as there are assassins to cut human lives off at the root, as long as the Messiah remains captive somewhere in the jails of tyrants or in inattentive hearts, there will be dybbuks or, if you will, rebels to refuse Babylon in the name of nomadic love which impels everyone toward everyone else.

This theme of the dybbuk is not, moreover, a gratuitous invention of the Jewish imagination, it is a very close description of what happens within man: the good personage, the angel assassinated because it was love, returns furtively every day to remind us that it is necessary to say no to the social order. Oh, good dybbuk, resting in my innermost depths, give me the courage to become you.

NOTES

1. In the "sacred" texts which are rightly considered the most sublime in the Bible, such as Job or the "Second Isaiah" (Isaiah, Chapter 40 to the end), Yahweh again becomes, if I dare say so, Elohim. The universality of Israel's mission, the abandonment of any specific nationalism, the purity of monotheism, the exigency of strength of soul and sincerity of heart have their most complete expression in these texts; one must remember that the anonymous prophet hidden behind this "Second Isaiah" wrote in exile, toward the end of the Babylonian captivity. This admirable prophet deserves humanity's eternal gratitude; he is the first to have said that all peoples have the same God, that one can honor this God only by being just, and that the idea that he can have a "house" (Isaiah 66) is absurd. Jonah will even be given the order, which would have stupified a cleric of the old school, to go and covert Nineveh (Jon. 3:2)!

2. Martin Buber (*Moses: The Revelation and the Covenant* [New York: Harper & Row, 1958] p. 13 ff.) does not in the least believe that this hypothesis, however frequently accepted, of the duality Yahwism and Elohism, is scientifically founded. Agreed. So what? Ernest Renan (trans. J. H. Allen and E. W. Latimer, *History of the People of Israel*, 5 vols. [Boston: Robert Brothers, 1888–96] especially in the first book, chaps. 2–12) takes it up again only to expand it, giving it an idealistic and postromantic interpretation. The margin between this and the religious vision is infinitesimal, if not non-existent.

That Renan takes the opposition as historically true and Buber as historically false means only that each, by placing himself in the sphere of history as science, prevents himself from dreaming, from using the Bible in that dream and that dream in life.

3. I have often raised these questions with my friend Bernard Hercenberg who defended a brilliant thesis on biblical esthetics. Our opinions sometimes differ, but our passion is the same.

4. The objection will be raised that Zionism, and the existence of Israel for the past thirty years, contradict this idea. The answer, as some religious people agree, is that the renunciation of a constant principle of Judaism is both a condition for and a result of the establishment of this State. Of course, why not? There have been waves of

conversions to Judaism and then there have been contrary waves of assimilation. Zionism and the State of Israel will perhaps be included among the latter.

5. For example, for the festival of Pesach (Passover), the symbolic sacrifice of the pascal lamb and eating matzo, that is, azymous or unleavened bread, are specifically ordained. The sacrifice of the lamb represents a nomadic civilization of shepherds and the unleavened bread symbolizes a later society of sedentary farmers. (Cf. J. Gutwirth, "Les pains azymes de la Pâque chez les hassidim," *Objets et mondes*, vol. 16, fasc. 4, [1976], p. 137 ff.) These two traditions are not successive, but juxtaposed. Besides, the unleavened bread itself is, in a manner of speaking, agricultural and sedentary by its content, flour, and nomadic because time was not taken to let it rise on the spot, as it was necessary to flee in order to escape servitude. The unleavened bread of Passover is a sign that a permanent danger threatens us, that security is always illusory and precarious. But better liberty than good bread. If consumer societies think about this adage, perhaps they will realize better bad bread than dead.

6. In Judaism, the initial letter possesses many properties. For this reason, there existed a sort of literary game which consists of beginning each sentence of each stanza with the letters of the

alphabet, in Cadmean order. Psalm 37 and the poem of the virtuous woman (Prov. 31:10) are two applications of this principle. The interminable Psalm 99, dedicated to praise of the Law, is an acrostic with the twenty-two letters of the alphabet, each repeated eight times.

7. Linguists call a text whose content is created by being stated "performative." If I say "the cherries are ripe," that does not make them ripen. But if the chairman of a meeting says "the meeting is open" (or "closed"), by this speech alone the meeting is opened or closed. Thus there is a supposition that the person who delivers a performative discourse has a certain power to which he refers, should the occasion arise ("in the name of the powers vested in me . . ."). So the idea alluded to here, that the personal name of God might be the Torah itself, that is the law that God decrees, is not surprising. In short, on Mt. Sinai, God would simply have named Himself to Moses.

I am much more shocked by the idea that God can have a name, like you and me. To be sure, one gives a name to a "noble" being: to a man, a boat, a house, a dog; if need be, to a duck. That means, too, that none of these beings is the sole of its species, since one names it to distinguish it. But God . . .

8. To transform an obstacle into a method is a familiar process in Freudian thought. Breuer had

fled panic-stricken when one of his patients, Anna O., who had fallen in love with him, flung her arms around his neck. Freud takes the problem up again on the theoretical level, works out the concept of transference and comes to the conclusion that the transference to the analyst of the long-standing basic feelings of the patient must be analyzed: in this way a working tool essential to the cure is discovered. Transference is transformed from an obstacle, which risked putting the doctor on the defensive, into an implement of therapy.

Countless things could be pointed out about the often contradictory and ambiguous relationship between Freud and Judaism. There is a whole literature on the matter.

It is indispensable to begin with the fact that Sigmund Freud, born into a Jewish family in which he had molded his character in *difference*, had been a brilliant pupil of Viennese schools, in *assimilation*. The notion of Oedipus refers explicitly to ancient Greek culture, the permanent search for foundations is connected to Jewish thought. Similarly, the idea is found in the Bible that the personality of certain individuals is defined by personal tendencies (often expressed by their proper name) which, in adulthood, are put to use in some socially or morally useful—and for them privileged—activity. Here is the concrete content of the idea of sublimation. The concern with efficacy, even the very idea of curing neuroses are more amenable to positivism, and more generally to non-Jewish thought.

Based on considerations of this sort, it could be concluded that Sigmund Freud represents a typical figure—and not among the least important—of what Jewish thought and the situation of a Jewish thinker "in diaspora" can bring to the world. Ultimately, thinking and especially rethinking foundations is an activity which is at one and the same time integrated and unintegrated into the social being in his totality. Integrated because one thinks of objects, beings, their relationships; in a word, of the world. Unintegrated because the world functions, or thinks it functions, without being thought. "Dreamwork does not think," said Freud, for example. This situation of the tension and paradox is both as if symbolized and empirically incarnated by the presence of Judaism in the universe where the diasporic destiny is realized. The messianic theme, with all its absurdity, paradox, paranoia and scandal, would here find a concrete content certainly never dreamt of by the authors of the Bible. These ironies are sometimes called history.

9. Bruno Zevi, "Judaïsme et conception spatiotemporelle en art," *Dispersion et Unité*, no. 14, Jerusalem (1975), p. 128 ff. I agree completely with this insightful Italian esthetician, a professor of the history of architecture at the University of Venice. This article is the text of a lecture

delivered in Italian on the occasion of the 9th Congress of the Italian Jewish community, 9 June 1974.

10. See, for example, Pierre Clastres' book, *Society Against the State*, trans. Robert Hurley (New York: Urizen Books, 1977). The author's pages on the Tupi-Guaranis (pp. 181–86) could apply word for word to the Hebrews. For the Tupi-Guaranis had their *nabis*, their prophets, who were called the Karaï and who were opposed to the establishment of a centralized power. The people preferred suicidal migration. On the other hand, a utopian philosopher like Martin Buber can consider that the State, at least if transformed into pure administration, is necessary to society. He said so in a lecture he gave at the 25th anniversary of the Hebrew University of Jerusalem, and published under the title "Society and the State" in *Pointing the Way: Collected Essays*, ed. & trans. with an introduction by Maurice Friedman (New York: Harper & Bros., 1957), pp. 161–76.

11. Theodor W. Adorno, *Asthetische Theorie* (Frankfurt am Main: Suhrkamp Verlag, 1970).

12. According to Hegel, the "first free men" in the Greek world were the sceptics, for in asserting that man's mental representations are perhaps not identical to the things represented, they declare the existence of a distance between per-

ception and things. (See, e.g., *Phenomenology of Spirit*, trans. A. V. Miller [New York: Oxford University Press, 1977], pp. 119–38.) Is it necessary to point out yet again that the Greeks excel in epistemology, and the Hebrews in ethics?

13. Robert Jaulin, in *Les Chemins du Vide* (Paris: Christian Bourgois, 1977), a book in which he evaluates the failure of civilizations, speaks of Jewish thought as a conception of the finality of history; in that sense, it would not be nomadism; one knows where one is going. But, on the other hand, the author shows that Israel has never finished going forth from Egypt, the Exodus remains to be made, the desert is still to be crossed. It is continually necessary to leave Pharaoh. Moses renews and extends Abraham. Robert Jaulin's thought can be interpreted in this way. See, too, Abraham Heschel's admirable book devoted to "the art of mastering time" in Judaism, *Les Bâtisseurs du temps* (Paris: Minuit, 1978).

THE NOMAD ABRAHAM

Judaism, Islam and Christianity take Abraham as a model of obedience to God, and the high point of his life as the moment when he must sacrifice his son Isaac—his sole legitimate descendant—and submit to God's will until, at the last moment, God retracts his decision. He had only been putting Abraham to the test.

In fact, matters are richer and more subtle. First of all, Abraham is a man of neither *unconditional* obedience nor submissiveness. He receives God's commandments sometimes calmly, sometimes rebelliously, sometimes with distress and uneasiness, so that the numerous episodes of Abraham's life must be more closely examined.

For the moment, let us settle for remembering that Abraham's nephew, Lot, who had gone to settle in Sodom, found himself in danger when the Eternal undertook to chastise that city of shame. Learning of that threat, Abraham, knowing that Lot led a virtuous life, undertook to convince God not to punish the good along with the evil; in one of the most extraordinary passages of the Bible (Gen. 18:23–24), Abraham asks God, "Wilt thou also destroy the righteous with the wicked? / Peradventure there be fifty righteous within the city." A negotiation with God follows (through Gen. 18:33), in the course of which Abraham "nibbles away" at the number of the righteous below which God will exercise the collective punishment on the criminal city. Holding to the letter of the text, one has the right to assume that without Abraham's intervention, God would have created an injustice, or to imagine that He could have committed one. Here again, God needs man. If only to inform Him that there are, despite everything, some righteous people in Sodom, for God Himself says that His only information is a "cry" (Gen. 18:20) and that He will go to see exactly what is occurring (Gen. 18:21). Further on, but still in the story of Abraham, Abimelech will take up the question addressed to God: "Wilt thou slay also a righteous nation?" (Gen. 20:4).

For 3000 years, structures more or less hidden in the biblical narrative have been looked for and found. Some are almost obvious (cf. *supra*, note 6). With respect to the story of Abraham, it presents what musicians call a "bridge structure," that is to say one whose constituent elements develop in a certain order from the beginning to the middle of the series; then, after this "middle," again in inverse order until the end. In music this would be, for example, *fa, sol, la, ti, la, sol, fa,* if the series included an odd number of elements; seven, in this case. It is conceivable that the last element in a narrative might be the strict repetition (*reprise,* in musical terms) of the first, the next to the last that of the second, the antepenultimate that of the third, and so forth. But it is equally conceivable that the elements thus paired be analogous but not identical. That is the case with the story of Abraham. The life of this patriarch, as it is reported in Genesis, from chapter 12, verse 1 to chapter 22, verse 24, is broken down into *ten* events which are in order, the following:

1. Abram must separate himself from his father (12:1)
2. Sarai is threatened by Pharaoh (12:15)
3. Abram must separate himself from Lot (13:9)
4. Lot is in danger (14:12)
5. Will Abram have a son? The birth of Ishmael (16:4); Here, in the middle, Abram changes his name to Abraham (17:5)
6. Will Abraham have another son? The

birth of Isaac (17:19); Sarai ("my princess") becomes Sarah ("the princess") (17:15)

7. Lot is again in danger (19:5)

8. Sarah is again threatened, this time, by Abimelech (20:2)

9. Abraham must, once again, separate himself from his loved ones, this time from Hagar and Ishmael (21:10)

10. Abraham again sees his line in danger of being broken; this time, it is in having to sacrifice Isaac (22:2)

First observation: one sole exception exists in all this, to the bridge structure: it is with regard to episodes 2 and 3, and 8 and 9. Two "ought" to correspond to 9 and 3 to 8; in fact, 2 corresponds to 8 and 3 to 9. But the sequence 2–3 does, indeed, correspond to the sequence 8–9. It is as though, instead of having: *fa, sol, la, ti, do, do, ti, la, sol, fa*, we had: *fa, sol–la, ti, do, do, ti, sol–la, fa.* Why?

Second observation: when the sequence includes an even number of elements, the one in the middle is repeated between the end of the forward half-series and the beginning of the half-series in inverse order. That is the case here, where we have *ten* elements. The repetition of episodes 5 (the birth of Ishmael) and 6 (the birth of Isaac) is most striking; the illegitimate son, with Hagar, the servant; the legitimate son, with Sarah, the wife. Now, it is precisely at this moment of the most obvious repetition of the narrative that the very name of the hero, by a repetition of the center of the word, changes from Abram to Abraham. The latter name, moreover, means "father of a multitude."

The first idea so strongly marked a structure brings to mind is that it is a mnemonic construction and, thus, a means of letting a narrator know, at the end of each episode, the next episode to which he must devote the sequel of his narrative.

Please remember here that the bridge structure of the story of Abraham is not the only one of its kind in Genesis: the order of creation, in seven days, is also constructed as a "bridge." The seventh day, that of rest, corresponds to the first, that of light. The sixth day, when the animals were created, corresponds to the second day, when the heaven and the earth were created, and so forth. The middle, unique because seven is an odd number, is the fourth day, when the sun, moon and stars were created. But this fourth day "chimes," too, in its way, with the first: to begin with, on each of the days there is only one creative act, whereas there are several on the other days; then, on those two days, God does not turn His attention directly to the Earth, but to what bathes or surrounds it.

Numerous other structures, countless other correspondences can be found, have been found, in the texts of the Torah and chiefly in Genesis. Jewish mysticism saw symbols to be deciphered and meanings to be discovered in these correspondences. The hermeneutic apparatus developed on this subject quickly became so subtle that the more complicated the deciphering techniques became, the less credible were the interpretations. But there are other possible hypotheses than that of a code message, notably the hypothesis of mnemonics, which here would take the form of a half-veiled, half-visible structure. Or, seeing it from a different angle, it is astonishing that the biblical narrative is so easy to retain that, from the start, several billion human beings, although they were, for the most part, illiterate and had no culture but the content of these texts, were able to assimilate at least its essence. How was this possible? Perhaps because these texts were, from the outset, constructed according to simple, sound schemata to give the memory something to fasten on and because, by means of repetition and differentiation, and glances forward (forecasts, predictions) and backward (reminders, repetitions, recurrence of analogous situations), they created in *time*, the dimension where the nomads moved, guideposts and reference points and techniques those without a fixed and limited *space* would otherwise lack.

This leads to the question of the transition from the oral to the written myth. It is conceivable that a mnemonically structured narrative might typically be an object of oral narration. A written narrative needs no mnemonics but the text itself: the written text preserves and transmits, whatever its internal arrangement. Here, one could meditate on the fact that, with all due deference to philosophers, human memory is a function which, itself, has a history. Preeminently a function of time, it is subject, too, to that which it aims to master. It is the mother as well as the daughter of history. We know that the despot of preclassical Greek civilization had, in his retinue, a servant, the *mnemon*, who had to remember all the episodes of the king's life and remind him of them at the proper time: the division of psychic functions was then a division of social roles. If ethnologists point out undeniable structural analogies among the myths of a people, of a century, of more than one continent, that is perhaps, on the one hand, because one of the most widely prevalent characteristics of human memory is precisely the formal element of myth and, on the other hand, because there are not infinite possible structures. Here again the last word of the structure would be its genesis, its history: *bereshit*.

If this hypothesis of a memorizable structure of the oral narrative were to be even partially verified, one could consider the possibility that the most structured texts predate their transcription and go back to a literally immemorial, that is, undatable, past, although, on the other hand, they are, in their way, its memory. The sole landmarks in time are its works themselves, in the broadest sense: a cyclical phenomenon, like the passage of the sun in front of a certain constellation, or a unique phenomenon like the black cloud over Egypt (in 1240 B.C.?), described in Exodus (10:22), and which resulted from the fantastic explosion on the island of Santorini (Thêra). The idea that all of that could have occurred in the same order, but a billion years, for instance, earlier or later, is completely meaningless; it would assume temporal reference points outside time and its works; in a word, it spatializes time. Only the inveterately sedentary could elaborate, as did ancient stoicism, for example, the idea of the cyclical return of time, of a "great year." If nothing is narrated, if there is no memory and consequently no mnemonics, there is nothing, there are no longer social ties, no longer a society and perhaps as a result and at a certain moment of development, no longer the possibility of life, even of physical life. Certainly, the formation of a historical thought resulting in writing, in historiography, is linked to the State, and even constitutes one of its functions, whether it is a matter, as in Thucydides, of reflecting on the past misfortunes of the city, in order to avert their return, or a matter, as it was for the Gauls, Joan of Arc or Napoleon, of cultivating a founding justificatory myth. Power, at least certain forms of power, needs historiographers. Charlemagne needs Einhard, and Louis XIV, Racine.

But probably not all historiographies are an official function of the State. The innumerable myths gathered and studied by the ethnologists are, too, accounts of the group's past, narratives of its origins, and the Bible is merely one of them. However, if these narratives ensure the unity of the group at the same time they relate it, and if the Bible is largely devoted to these functions with respect to the human group of the Hebrews, it presents particular features which are well known. Monotheism is very obviously the most important, but not the sole, of these. The characteristic impotence of the State resulting on the theoretical level—and, for the Hebrews, on the practical level—from the fact that the link of the people to the divine concerns time rather than space, history rather than geography, is incomparably rich for our era. There is, indeed, a promised land, a promise effectively kept the day Moses showed this land to his people, but without going there himself. Robert Jaulin, we have seen, explains that Israel has never completely gone forth from Egypt. Please bear in mind now that, well before Moses, Abraham, too, had followed the itinerary, if not the same path, at least according to the same signposts. That is how nomads live, they are offered fewer journeys than at a tourist agency: two or, at the very most, three possible routes, dependent on needs dictated by natural resources, their exhaustion and regeneration, the seasons, the climates, the main roads, the stamina of the men and of the livestock, the areas populated by friends or enemies, and so on.

* * *

Here, following the mnemonic function of the bridge structure in the myth of Abraham, we arrive at an even richer meaning of his story.

Before his first adventure, Abram was sedentary; after his tenth adventure, which all but ended in the blood of his son, Abraham again became sedentary by settling in Hebron (always the same consonants) where he buried Sarah (Gen. 23:1–20). And if he accepted that a wife be sought for his son in the country from which he came, he forbade that his son himself be taken back there (24:6). The new land was prescribed to him by God (24:7). In summary, all of Abraham's "active" life, except his birth in Mesopotamia and his death on the land he had acquired to bury Sarah (25:10), is a nomadic life, in the course of which he had already chanced (13:18) to go to Hebron.

Now, what is decisive is the symbolic and

moral significance of the "nomadic arc" of his existence: there he is in contact with God. While this arc lasts, for example, God addresses Himself *directly* to Abraham several times, without the intermediary of a messenger. That is the case in 12:1–3; 15:1–21; 18:10, 13–14, 20–32; 22:1–2; whereas God addresses himself to other characters through the mediation of an emissary (e.g., 16:7–12, 19:1, 21:17–18). In fact, during this part of his existence, Abraham enjoys a special privilege, this direct contact with God, to the point where he is quite at ease with the special interventions of the Eternal, which no longer even surprise him. He expects them, he waits for them. That is the inestimable and irreplaceable privilege of the nomad: he is close to God, held tightly in His hand, he even is His hand. This marvelous contact is broken, lost, when man settles down somewhere in space, gets caught up in "worldly" tasks, where even God Himself can seek him only by availing Himself of other means, intermediaries, intercessors. Simplicity, purity and immediate presence are the specific attributes of nomadism, of those who have abandoned spatial tasks to dedicate themselves to God—that is, to time.

Abraham is generally presented as the symbol of obedience. This is not true. Abraham is grace, the gift of God (as Reuben, too, will be), just as Isaac is the symbol of severity, stability and respect for the law and for the precise details of the covenant between the people and the Eternal (as Simeon, too, will be). Abraham, after the long narrative which goes from the end of the flood (9:28) to his first act (12:1), constitutes the great new event, the first intervention of God after three centuries of a kind of indifference He showed man after the punishment of the flood. There are, in the Bible, dry periods, so to speak, and "hot spots"; there are moments when the narrative enumerates a chronology, a genealogy (e.g., here from 11:10–32) and then moments when something happens, and when the monotonous succession of generations makes way for a true chronicle.

The intervention of God, who, in 12:1, calls Abraham, bursts on the scene as an unexpected event; it has something of a *new creation*, it is a gift, it is grace: the gift of a remarkable ancestor, the gift of a double filiation (Ishmael and Isaac), from which everything starts all over again, the promise of descendants, the real beginning of the proper history of the people of Israel. Humanity comes out of its primitive gangue; it is going to take shape; millennia which might have been unheard of begin; they will never come to know, but will always wait for, the impossible Messiah. Abraham is at once the product, the symbol and the bearer of this gift, this creation of differentiated and specific peoples emanating from a onedimensional humanity, this gratuitous gesture of power and goodness, forethought and love. To say that Abraham "obeys" God is to define him by a relationship of dependency and passivity, which would leave room for fear or resignation, reticence or calculation, which would, in short, introduce a distance between God and His nomad. There is no such thing in the text: on the contrary, the nomad Abraham is so close to God, so steeped in His light, that he is quite naturally the agent of Providence, he is the one whose destiny literally does not depend on the superior will, but is identified with it absolutely. The *non pareo deo, sed assentior* of stoicism, the theoretical principle which is the end result of a system of concepts is here, in Genesis, an actual fundamental given, a concrete and dated historical event, which subsequently became a moral archetype. To make of Abraham a man who carries out orders, who obeys, and to present him to the Jewish, Christian and Islamic masses as a model of submission, is to misinterpret a message which effectively obstructs the power principle, distorting it to the advantage of the power and authority of one being over another. The message is in fact a message of liberty: the liberty of God, who is, if one dare say so, under no obligation to extricate the races from their monotonous repetition; and the liberty of Abraham, whom nomadic life withdraws from slavery to consecrate to the creative adventure until that other irremissible term of our liberty, death.

Abraham does not submit to God: *he is on His side*. He came over to it part and parcel the day he crossed the river: "Set free, set free," as the sermon of Benares puts it in another religion, "having reached the other bank, bring the others across." The fascination of the river.

That is what life is: leaving the original prison, clearing, transgressing the banks. Let us wander about quite a bit, seek we know not what, meet Sarah, the Princess, and love her; practice guile with Pharaoh, the State; fear for Lot, tremble and then quake with fear for Isaac; cry over Hagar and Ishmael; let us do all that until the day the earth takes hold of us. Abraham is the point on which all possible phantasms hinge, the pretext for all migrations. They are sanctioned by the very text of Genesis and then, in turn, they transgress it, remaining faithful to it in their fashion by betraying it, by using it as a basis for leading a nomadic life.

But what about the other aspect; what is there, not in the dream or delirium the text might engender, but in the harsh reality of the peoples that engendered it? There is, it is said, God. There are some who are satisfied with that, dwelling on it, going no further, setting up their church and petrifying their dreams there, fixing their thought at that exact point. But to do so is to forget the other specter which is not moral but material, haunting not man's mind but his stomach: famine. It, too, underlies all the texts of the Bible. The divine "grace" which draws Abram away from Ur is, in reality, hunger and the *hope* of escaping it. It is this impulse toward survival, this will to continue, this love of life which—in innumerable diverse forms—became the final cause, at once the beginning and the end of all Jewish thought. Closely linked with it is the joy of existence which, in Judaism, is always ready to burst forth. Popular Hassidism, in its time, was astonishing evidence of this joy which also indelibly distinguishes Yiddish humor, in the way it continually plays off a theoretical and theological principle against vital daily realities.

The Bible would be similar, were it not first and foremost, and in its own way, the extraordinary schema of all human history, formulated on the awareness of the actual situation of the species: one *may* think, one *may* dream, invent, narrate; but there is a prerequisite to all that: one *must* eat. If there is enough to meet one's needs, one stays. If there is no longer anything, one leaves. If there is nothing elsewhere, either, one tries to procure it for oneself in another way: "Abel was a keeper of sheep, but Cain was a tiller of the ground" (Gen. 4:2). It is the only option which can permit and protect all the rest: thought, love, plans, sorrow and joy. It is hope, that is, the impulse, the insurrection of subjectivity.

Sedentarization is what humanity has been constrained to by scarcity. It is, obviously, irreversible. Gathering fruits and hunting are no longer sufficient; it is necessary to produce, to force nature to generate what is needed. The price of that is the construction of cities, which sooner or later leads to the cult of idols. It is necessary to nourish one's body, but at the cost of losing one's soul. In the hope of saving it despite everything, ethics is invented. In regretful memory of the previous mentality that had to be abandoned, the Bible is written. Dreaming of a world where the materialistic city would function without crushing the individual and his values, where the "management of things" would not lead to the "government of men," men become stoics, Christians, Proudhonniens, romantics, positivists, Marxists, Trotskyites, Maoists or anarchists. But as the promised glorious revolutions betrayed rather than kept their promises, there is an attempt to understand everything *bereshit*, "in the beginning," and it is seen that idols, power and spatial domination are in league to uproot us from time and inwardness, that is to say, from our life itself. What Jeremiah and Isaac knew as though instinctively becomes clear: the contradiction between external power and internal joy is insoluble. One must, one can always choose. The only (reasonable?) hope one might have is that the choice be understood.

FINALE

For those without direct access to the text, reading the Bible involves putting one's trust in the translator. With the help of specialists of different religions, André Chouraqui has recently produced a French translation of the Bible (Paris: Desclée de Brouwer, 1975) that upsets generally accepted ideas and gives the strong impression, reinforced on every page, that the Bible is *also* a musical object.

What can be the meaning of this impression? In fact, there is, at the very core of music, an opposition between the principles of organization and the possibility or the temptation of breaching this organization.

The main point is, perhaps, that the principle of organization here represents the exterior of the subject and the improvisational impetus its inner life. By the traditions of the art, the structure is imposed first on the composer and then on his listeners, even if this principle is internalized, even if some subjectivity adheres to it. The other force, which leads to the transgression of forms (in the musical sense of the term), derives its justification from recourse to the "inner life," to sensitivity itself, to the radically romantic conception of the subject and of the music that that conception should engender. And romanticism was, in effect, a time of great upheaval of traditions in the name of inspiration.

When the work of music derives entirely from one or the other of these principles, the problem is not resolved, only eluded. Punctilious respect for the rules of organization, even if only to bring the rare and thus more striking transgressions into greater relief, as in classical music, reinforces the structures esthetically and socially, in such a way that the very possibility of recourse to a free radical form seems increasingly excluded. On the other hand, reference solely to the unforeseeable movements of the inner life tends to limit musical discourse to anecdotes, as in the later romantics, to impressions; unless liberation from the rules serves as a pretext to turn the musical matter back on the techniques of its own production, and then that becomes the trap of virtuosity.

What is at stake here is much more than the clearly essential question of styles and of schools; it is, in fact, a matter of the whole conception of music. Ideology is also charged with reintegrating musical improvisation into the social order by imposing reassuring structures on it, as well as with discrediting it, if necessary, by relegating it to pure subjectivity, which it incidentally deprives of substantiality and of presence. The only solution, then, is to take on the two exigencies at the same time, in the same musical discourse, and to find the narrow path where there is no yielding either to forms bequeathed by the art's past or to the vertigo of subjective decision acting as the sovereign judge of musical matter and discourse.

It is not a matter of keeping an equilibrium between both terms, or of seeking a compromise, but of working out solutions to the problem which would be both radical and really musical. As Adorno showed, and Boucourechliev fully confirmed, that is what Beethoven did and that is why he was seen as the major composer whose music must always be taken into account. In Beethoven, in fact, the always problematical unity between the work and the subject is again brought into question, realized and its problems seemingly easily mastered. This music thus has a decisive role, because it is situated between Haydn, in whose music the richest form of classical thought is realized, and Brahms, in whose music all power over the discourse is entrusted to the subject.

In Beethoven's chosen itinerary, the structure is dictated by the idea, not by tradition, nor by the systematic transgression of tradition. For example, the primordial role of the cello in the seventh quartet (Opus 59 No. 1) illustrates this point well: Beethoven does not paradoxically give this instrument the theme and derisively reduce the others to mere accompaniment, but creates a truly new relationship able to bring the cello out of its traditional function in order to satisfy a movement of pure subjectivity: the taste for a low pitch. Another example: Boucourechliev showed that the Diabelli Variations (Opus 120), owe their sparkling freshness both to an original strict construction and to the wish to explore, through the inclusion of a medley of typical examples, a wide range of possible past, present and future styles.

In other words, Beethoven's music is, at the same time and in the same movement, an opening to the law of time, which adds liberty and takes it away, exercises and annuls it, and a mastery and an awareness of that law, musically realized by the totally free use of the structural possibilities bequeathed by tradition.

Ultimately, a piece of music constructed entirely *a priori* and without being listened to could engender only repetition and boredom; on the other hand, a piece of music guided only by the inspiration of the moment would itself disappear like the instant which brought it, and to which, alone, it would have abandoned itself. It is known that consciousness unendowed with memory would continually annul itself and would literally not exist. Beethoven's endeavor is an imposing attempt to weave a net, not to retain time, but to make its passage perceptible without taking away any of its liberty; on the contrary, saving the liberty from nothingness by restoring it to us.

The Bible does exactly the same thing. To the undifferentiated flow of the centuries, the Bible opposes a history, an aggregate of dates, from the millennial past to the distant future, in which the destiny of the peoples will be inscribed; but this aggregate is conceived non-systematically, according to a rhythm which does not arbitrarily shape its content according to a pattern, but rather patterns itself on its content in such a way as to throw it into relief. For example, one of the major themes of Genesis, that of the sequence of generations is, in certain passages, developed, taken up again (reprised), differentiated, then shattered or temporarily thrust aside by the story of such and such a patriarch, only to be recovered later, in an altered but identifiable form, with all possible variations on names, ages, acts. This process recognizably follows, term by term, the definition of Beethoven's *Durchführung* or, as the approximate English equivalent puts it, the "development" of a theme: neither rigidity of structure, nor indifference of the structure to its content, nor a vision of history as the plaything of some capricious or delirious divinity. The world of the Bible is not God's nightmare: it is His will intermingled with the expression of that will. The time of music in Beethoven is not the internalization of a secret of his, it is the awareness of it organized into a communicable and referential language and thereby made universal, as is the Bible.

Thrust into an incomplete, ill-formed world without his consent, the human being has only his life, only his lifetime between two nothingnesses. Possessed, in fact, by what he thinks he possesses, ruled by what he dreams of ruling, generally destroyed by the salvations he counts on, he does not even have full enjoyment of the time he has, he is not conscious of being alive when he lets time be frittered away in oblivious instantaneousness. The only ethics that can respond to this situation are those that reject false solutions, the distractions of space, objects and idols. The biblical ethic, for example, or the musical ethic.

Music, which carves its own time out of the time of the universe, making it, as it were, present to itself by its specific perceptible qualities: rhythm, phrasing, movement, tempo, reprise, variation. . . . The Bible which, at one and the same time, narrates and circumscribes the time

of the world, and fills it not only with characters, with actions, with achievements, but also
with qualities focused on time, such as memory
and utopia, nostalgia and enterprise, adventure,
promise, self-abnegation, foresight. Fidelity, too.

The Bible and music give us back our lives
whereas idols rob us of them. The Bible and music give consistency to the image of that life, reflecting it directly at us. It is an image which is
at once derisory and pitiless, tortured and vain
and yet, when it is infiltrated by the perhaps evil,
but nevertheless irresistible, demons of love and
hope, its pulsation is fascinating to feel. Listen to
time slip by.